D1048260

# OVERHEARD IN DUBLIN

## DUBLIN WIT FROM OVERHEARDINDUBLIN.COM

Gill & Macmillan

Dedicated to Deirdre

We'd like to thank all those people who have posted overheard stories to our website. Without you, there would be no 'Overheard in Dublin'!

Gill & Macmillan Ltd
Hume Avenue, Park West, Dublin 12
with associated companies throughout the world
www.gillmacmillan.ie
© Gerard Kelly and Sinéad Kelly 2006
ISBN-13: 978 07171 4114 2
ISBN-10: 0 7171 4114 4
Print origination by TypeIT, Dublin
Illustrations by Eoin Coveney
Printed and bound by Nørhaven Paperback A/S,
Denmark

This book is typeset in 10pt Garamond Book on 11pt.

The paper used in this book comes from the wood pulp of managed forests. For every tree felled, at least one tree is planted, thereby renewing natural resources.

A CIP catalogue record for this book is available from the British Library.

5 4 3

# Marty Whel (of Fortune)

Was on the way home from the Ireland versus Sweden match last week on the DART when a random drunk spots Marty Whelan. A lot of banter went back and forward and then the drunk starts shouting at Marty, 'Wheel of Fortune'.

He was having so much fun and was loving the sound of his own voice so much I don't think anyone had the heart to tell him Marty hosts 'Fame and Fortune'.

Overheard by Ali, northbound DART
Posted on Tuesday, 7 March 2006

# Ray D'Arcy crisps

Walking down Nassau Street the other day, I was passing a billboard ad for Walkers crisps (it's just a picture of Gary Lineker holding a bag of crisps). Two D4 type girls were walking in front of me. On seeing the picture:

Girl#1: 'Why is there a picture of Ray D'Arcy holding a bag of crisps?'

Girl#2: 'I dunno, it's a bit stupid alright isn't it?'

… I agree, there's an awful lot of stupid going around.

Overheard by Val, Nassau Street
Posted on Monday, 6 March 2006

## Smelly bum

On the bus a while ago. A rather large woman with a bit of a B.O. problem gets on. Cue little boy, sniffing, 'Wot's dat smell? Wot's dat smell!'

His mam tries to get him to shut up. No luck. He continues, 'I tink it's her (pointing to the large woman). Yeah, it's her. She's got a smelly bum!'

Needless to say, that's when the mam chose to get off the bus.

Overheard by CC, no. 3 bus
Posted on Friday, 3 March 2006

## Hong Kong Elvis

A girl in work said she has an Elvis CD that you can only buy in Hong Kong. One of her fellow employees asked,

'What's it called, wok and roll?"

Genius!

Overheard by Anonymous, George's Quay
Posted on Friday, 3 March 2006

# A Crumblin poet

Sitting outside Redz on Thursday night. A young one and this fella were having a chat.

Girl: 'Where ye from?'

Fella: 'Crumblin. Where ye from?'

Girl: 'Ballyfermot.'

Fella replies, 'Ballyfermot people pick your pockets!' Turns to walk away, shouting, 'Watch yer pockets, boys, Ballyer Birds in the House!'

Leaving a very shocked girl on the corner of O'Connell Street.

Overheard by Mary, Redz, O'Connell Bridge
Posted on Thursday, 2 March 2006

# Get out more!

I used to work in a pub in Lucan (where everybody thinks they're a D4 head) and here was the order I got one night:

'Pint of the black stuff (fair enough), pint of Heino (right so), a Shirley Bassey (we'll get to that in a minute), and a bottle of apples.' (Figured it out?)

Here is a legend of what they all translate to:

Pint of the black stuff — Guinness (obviously)
Pint of Heino — Heineken (obviously)
Shirley Bassey — Black Bush
Bottle of apples — Bulmers

When we say that these people need to get out more, it doesn't mean go out and upset the bar staff of their local!

Overheard by Matt, in work, pub in Lucan
Posted on Thursday, 2 March 2006

## Kennedy's brain

Listening to 'What's in Kennedy's Head', the prestigious game show on FM104, whereby listeners have to guess what Adrian Kennedy (host of the above game show) is thinking of — i.e., what's in his head — by asking him clues.

Cue the nice lady with the accent straight out of Moore Street, whose question was, 'Is it something in your head?' And who then proceeded to guess, 'Is it your brain?'

It wasn't.

Overheard by David, FM104
Posted on Wednesday, 1 March 2006

## A plaice without sole!

While my friend was in a pub he took a picture of some classic graffitti on the wall in the bathroom, saying, 'A city without a chipper is a plaice without sole.'

Good to see there are some poets left in Dublin!

Overheard by Naomi, city centre pub
Posted on Tuesday, 28 February 2006

## Funny riot!

Overheard at the riots in town on Saturday:

'Stones five for 50, Helmets €1'

Ah, the Dublin humour even in times of strife!

Overheard by Linda, O'Connell Street
Posted on Tuesday, 28 February 2006

# Rioters

Conversation between two masked rioters on Saturday:

Rioter #1: 'Did ya hear me sister's having twins?'

Rioter #2: 'No way, dat's brilliant ...'

And then they continued to fire rocks at the police ... classic Dublin.

Overheard by Steff, O'Connell Street
Posted on Tuesday, 28 February 2006

# Leinster House moves to Dame Street

Three scumbags running over O'Connell Bridge during the riots.

Scumbag #1: 'Leg it, we gotta geh to Leinster House.'

Scumbag #2: 'Where's dat?'

Scumbag #3: 'Down be Dame Street.'

Overheard by Dan, O'Connell Bridge
Posted on Monday, 27 February 2006

# Drinks round

I used to work in a busy city centre bar and I once got the following order from a customer (of D4 persuasion):

'Hi, could I have a Heino, a Probs, an AG, a VRB, a JDC and a GT.'

AKA: A Heineken, a Carlsberg, a Guinness (as in Arthur Guinness), a vodka and Redbull, a Jack

Daniels and Coke, and a Gin and Tonic (that one's fair game).

Overheard by Amy, pub, Dublin 2
Posted on Monday, 27 February 2006

## I predict a riot

A man loudly shouts into his mobile phone on the Saturday afternoon of the Love Ulster parade riots:

'I'm going down to O'Connell Street to throw a few bricks at the coppers.'

Overheard by Swench, Exchequer Street, Dublin 2
Posted on Saturday, 25 February 2006

## Use the sink!

While in Mother Redcaps pub I overheard this girl who returned from the ladies toilet saying to her friends, 'I don't like washing my hands in that toilet.'

Quick as a flash the barman said, 'Most people use the sink.'

Overheard by Max, Mother Redcaps
Posted on Thursday, 23 February 2006

## Ballymunners

Written on the back of the no. 77A bus:

'Ballymunners rob yer runners.'

Overheard by John, no. 77A bus
Posted on Thursday, 23 February 2006

# An offer you can refuse

Seen, not heard. Poster in hairdresser's window, offering a root-dyeing service for people whose highlights were starting to grow out:

'Come in and let us touch you up.'

Overheard by Flan, Hair-braid shop, Marlborough Street,
Parnell Street
Posted on Tuesday, 21 February 2006

# Babyface O'Reilly

A group of boys were hanging around a small park in Dublin 12. Another teenage boy rides up on a flash pushbike.

Small boy: 'Where did you rob that?'

Teen: 'Didn't. I bought it.'

Small boy: 'Nah, you couldn't'a. Where'd you rob it?'

Teen: 'I told you I bought it at [cycle shop].'

Small boy: 'And here I thought you were some sort of gangster. What kind of gangster does that?'

Overheard by Anonymous, St Martin's Drive, Dublin 12
Posted on Saturday, 18 February 2006

# Sectarian songs

Was busking in Temple Bar late last Saturday night. A group of lads, total Dubs, came up and started singing with me. One of them turned to me and asked me to play 'some sectarian songs'! His friends got very enthusiastic. 'Yeah play some sectarian songs!'

I didn't, and I didn't play any racist or anti-Semitic songs either!

Overheard by Anonymous, Temple Bar
Posted on Friday, 17 February 2006

## The ref's ma ...

Standing on Hill 16 at a Dublin match, when the referee made a terrible call. A guy shouts out, 'Ref, do ye know hew bleedin ugly yer ma is?' He continues, '… she's so bleedin ugly, she couldn't gerra DART in Connolly Station!'

Everyone was in hysterics.

Overheard by JG, Hill 16
Posted on Tuesday, 14 February 2006

## Strawberries

On a school trip from the North down to Dublin there was a Dub selling strawberries. 'Stra-brees, stra-brees,' she shouted. My friend from Tyrone turned to me and asked, 'What did she say?' And before I had a chance to answer, my other friend said, 'Er, something about a strong breeze.'

Overheard by Carmel, Grafton Street
Posted on Monday, 13 February 2006

# High four!

I was cycling home from work the other day, and as I passed a packed bus stop a woman put her hand out to stop the bus. The cyclist in front of me slapped her hand while shouting 'High Five!'

The girl, with a rather heavy Dublin accent, screamed after him, while holding her fingers in the air, 'I've only got four fingers you bastard!'

The people standing at the bus stop erupted with laughter.

Overheard by Pablo, bus stop outside Connolly DART Station
Posted on Thursday, 9 February 2006

# Vicious words

Scribbled on the no. 13 bus stop on O'Connell Street:

'Finglas heads wet their beds.'

Overheard by Brian.K, no. 13 bus stop on O'Connell Street
Posted on Wednesday, 1 February 2006

# Gotta know the lingo around here!

Security guard, foreign national probably Nigerian, gesturing with his walkie-talkie to dealer bloke to tidy up pallets and boxes near shopping centre doorway.

Dealer: 'Der's no problem, mate. Get yer gaffer on the blower and I'll have a chinwag wih 'im, he knows the jackanory.'

Retreats one very confused security guard!

Overheard by Anonymous, Ilac entrance, Moore Street
Posted on Tuesday, 24 January 2006

# Kittens ... fussy little bastards!

One day I was too lazy to go shopping so I decided to do an on-line Superquinn order rather than having to get ready and drive in traffic etc. While ordering my groceries I realised I had no kitten food so I added two boxes of Whiskas Kitten to my order.

Later on I received a phone call from Superquinn saying there were a few things they were out of stock on ... one of which was the kitten food. Here's the conversation:

Girl: 'We're out of the kitten food ... would de Adult wan be OK?'

Me: 'Ah no, sure, I'll leave it.'

Girl: 'Are ye sure? I have de Wiskis Adult food here.'

Me: 'No, really it's OK cos they're only three months old they can't eat the Adult food.'

Girl: [Thinks for a few seconds] 'Wha abou the Kite Kat Adult ... will dey eat da?'

Me: 'No, honestly it's OK they're only kittens.'

Girl: 'Jaysus, dem cats, fussy little bastards aren't they!'

Overheard by catlady, on the phone to Superquinn
Posted on Friday, 20 January 2006

# The honesty of a schoolboy

In a school science class a 'well built' female teacher was talking about heat travelling from one thing to another.

Teacher: 'And what would happen if I sat down on this radiator, boys?'

Student: 'You'd break it miss!'

It was worth him getting suspended for — we laughed for hours after.

*Overheard by daithi, a school that shall remain un-named!*
*Posted on Friday, 20 January 2006*

## Irish generosity ...

Saw a sign above a promotional 'offer' in a Centra:

'Buy one, get one!'

So typical of Ireland today …

*Overheard by Paul, Centra beside Temple Bar*
*Posted on Thursday, 19 January 2006*

## Motor tax problems

While in the motor tax office in Nutgrove I overheard a woman who was struggling to fill in her motor tax renewal form ask her friend, 'How the fecking hell are you supposed to remember the chastity number?'

*Overheard by Sinead, Motor Tax Office, Nutgrove*
*Posted on Wednesday, 18 January 2006*

## Drunken philosophy

Written inside one of the ladies toilets in The Bleeding Horse on Camden Street:

'Seriously, the hokey pokey, really what is it all about?'

*Overheard by Anonymous, The Bleeding Horse*
*Posted on Wednesday, 18 January 2006*

# Bus aerobics

On the bus heading out of town an elderly woman in a wheelchair is wheeled on by her husband. She asks him to wheel her further down the bus, and he says, 'We're only staying on for two stops, will ye just sit there,' to which she replies nice and calmly with an auld Dub twang, 'Well I'm not going to get up and do aerobics around the bus, am I?'

Overheard by SC, no. 20B bus
Posted on Saturday, 14 January 2006

# Raffle ticket

Overheard in the Hole In The Wall pub, raffle ticket seller from local GAA club is selling tickets. He approaches a drunk at the bar.

'Do you want to buy a raffle ticket?'

'Is it for the local GAA club?' replies the drunk.

'No,' says the ticket seller, 'it's for a portable telly and a feckin ham … do you want one or wha?'

Overheard by Anonymous, Hole In The Wall, Blackhorse Avenue
Posted on Tuesday, 10 January 2006

# Clever blonde

Blonde, sitting in an office in Ballymount where she has worked for the last eight months, asks: 'Where is Dublin 12?'

Manager: 'You've been working in it for the last eight months.'

Overheard by Matt, office in Ballymount, Dublin 12
Posted on Tuesday, 10 January 2006

# Sharon's OK, no cause for concern

Standing in the queue at a sandwich bar in town. There's a TV monitor on the wall to keep the queue folk from getting restless. Sky News is on with no sound, and the main story and newsflash info bar are regarding Israeli Prime Minister Ariel Sharon's health. The headlines strap line reads, 'Sharon's health declines further'. Two girls in front of me seem baffled by this and one says to the other, 'Who's Sharon, is she the one from X Factor, Osbourne, what happened her?'

I nearly wet myself, but had to step in when they kept questioning each other, making assumptions about what could have happened.

'He's the Israeli Prime Minister,' I said.

To which the same girl replied, 'Ah, sure then I don't care.'

Celebrity vs Politics, brilliant. Brightened up my January no end.

Overheard by Larry, Rathmines Inn
Posted on Thursday, 5 January 2006

# Pot kettle black

At the Leinster v Munster Rugby match, I overheard a Munster fan shouting at the Leinster players, 'You're a bunch of langers!'

Overheard by Tim, RDS
Posted on Wednesday, 4 January 2006

# Mr Happy at Glenageary Station

Me: 'Can you tell me the time of the next train to Greystones?'

Glenageary ticket clerk: 'The wallllll!'

Me: 'Excuse me, the wallllll? I want to know the time of the next train to Greystones.'

Glenageary ticket clerk: 'The wallllll!'

Me: 'The wallllll … what's a wallllll?'

Glenageary ticket clerk: 'The wallllll! The wallllll! Timetable … (on) the wallllll!'

Overheard by Damian, at Glenageary Railway Station
Posted on Wednesday, 4 January 2006

# Mothers, ya gotta love em!

During a very distressing situation, my mother was faced with a man who entered her workplace, threatening to burn the place to the ground. He had some petrol with him and began to pour the contents about the place. My mother immediately pushed a panic button, alerting the guards, and all was fine in the end.

However, later on while talking about the ordeal with my sister, she came out with this gem:

My sister: 'So, Mam, how did you react so fast, I mean, was it the adrenalin?'

My mother amazingly replies, 'No, no, it was definitely the petrol!'

Overheard by Graeme, at home in Dublin
Posted on Thursday, 29 December 2005

# Dry or greasy skin, sir?

At a beautician in Stillorgan, I ran into an old friend buying his girlfriend's Christmas present — some fancy moisturiser. After much thought he picked up one of the numerous varieties of moisturiser and brought it to the counter. Still unsure, he sought advice from the lady behind the counter:

Guy: 'Pardon me, but do you think this is a good moisturiser for my girlfriend?'

Lady: 'Well that depends, what type of skin does she have?'

Guy: 'I dunno … Caucasian?!'

Overheard by darkhorse, Stillorgan
Posted on Thursday, 29 December 2005

# Male or female?

In school a few years ago, a very well-spoken teacher was getting us to fill out a form. In a very clear and loud voice he said, 'Now where it says sex, do not write yes please or no thank you.'

Cue uproarious laughter from the entire year.

Overheard by Wilbo, southside school
Posted on Thursday, 22 December 2005

# The important issues of the day

While sitting upstairs on the no. 77 bus (air full of hash smoke as usual) we pass by the new Lidl supermarket on the Greenhills Road.

Stoned guy #1: 'Look ders de new Lidl!'

Stoned guy #2: 'Ah yeah, der popping up everywhere.'

Stoned guy #1: 'Is it Liddle or Leedle or Loidle?'

(They ponder on this for a couple of seconds.)

Stoned guy #2: 'I dunno but I know de other one's called Aldi.'

Stoned guy #1: 'Anyway the beer's durt cheap it is …'

Overheard by G, no. 77 bus
Posted on Wednesday, 21 December 2005


## Frozen

There were a few lads working in the frozen section of Dunnes Stores, throwing frozen turkeys into the fridge with some force, when some old dear turns around to them and says, 'Ah be careful with them turkeys, boys, they'll bruise when they thaw out.'

To which a reply came, 'Don't worry about it, luv, they can't feel a thing …'

Overheard by Orlando, Dunnes Stores
Posted on Tuesday, 20 December 2005


## Using your head

In college, the angry janitor was trying to push some kind of trolley past everyone in the canteen queue, but no one was paying any attention to him.

Janitor: 'Sorry, sorry, excuse me, excuse me …'

No one is listening.

Janitor: 'Jaysus, ah look, ders €20 on the ground.'

Everyone looks towards the imaginary money.

Janitor: 'Yiz f\*\*kin heard that!'

Overheard by John, Ballyfermot College

Posted on Sunday, 18 December 2005

# Sick bus?

Man to bus driver: 'Is this bus going to the Mater Hospital?'

Bus driver: 'Well, I dunno, it was fine when I took it ourra da garage dis morning ...'

Overheard by Nicantuile, Chapelizod, Dublin

Posted on Saturday, 17 December 2005

# Everyday Luas talk

On the Luas a group of 15–16 year old boys coming from school got on at Bluebell. One of them complained to his mates that his girlfriend had dumped him the night before by text! Highly indignant at this insult he said he was better off without her anyway; all she was doing was costing him money. He went on to detail all the money he had spent on her, bringing her out and buying her presents.

'I must have spent at least €400 on her,' he announced to his mates, at which one of them piped up, 'Jaysus for that kind of money I'll be your girlfriend.'

Overheard by Anonymous, Luas to Tallaght
Posted on Monday, 12 December 2005

# Viva le euros

While at the bureau de change in the Bank of Ireland this old lady in front of me went to the counter and said to the girl behind the desk, 'Hello love, I'm going to France this weekend so I just want to change my Irish euros into French euros.'

Overheard by Sean, Bank of Ireland, Tallaght
Posted on Thursday, 8 December 2005

# Is there a doctor in the house?

In the Omniplex a while back, a particularly boring bit of the movie was on, when a cry came from the dark.

Shadow at the front (shouting): 'Anyone! Is there

a doctor here? Is there a doctor here?'

(Shock. Confusion.)

Voice from the back: 'Here, I'm a doctor.'

Voice from the front: 'Sh*te film, isn't it?' ... and sat back down.

Voice from the back: 'Little bastard, if I find ya I'll rattle ya.'

Overheard by YoYoBoy, Santry Cinema
Posted on Sunday, 5 December 2005

## A delicate legal matter

In Court No. 4 at the Four Courts, a woman who alleged a serious verbal assault was in the witness box, and was asked by defence counsel, 'Can you tell the court what the defendant said?'

Woman: 'I'm a respectable woman; I couldn't possibly say those words in public.'

Kindly judge: 'Perhaps it might preserve everyone's dignity if the witness wrote the alleged word on a piece of paper.'

Having been given the piece of paper and a pen, the woman still appeared to be in difficulty, and the judge intervened to ask her, 'Is everything alright?'

To which the redoubtable Dublin woman replied, 'Is there one or two 'l's in bollix?'

Overheard by Gary, Court No. 4 at the Four Courts
Posted on Saturday, 4 December 2005

## Sound as a euro

Man shouts over to elderly woman in a bar in Ballyfermot, 'How's it going there, Patsy, keeping well?' to which the woman replied loudly,

'Sound as a euro, sound as a euro.'

Overheard by Anna, Ballyfermot
Posted on Saturday, 4 December 2005

## French literature for dummies

On the way home from work on the no. 46A bus. It's packed, it's hot and everyone is well and truly pissed off (including the driver). The UCD stop comes up and the bell rings. Then the bell rings again and again and again and again. Obviously each person getting off thought they were the first to do it. Suddenly the bus driver slams on the brakes, turns on the intercom and roars at the entire bus …

'Will yis stop ringing the bleedin' bell, who the f**k do yis think I am? I'm not f**kin Quasimodo!'

Overheard by Jessica, on the no. 46A bus
Posted on Saturday, 4 December 2005

## AIB security doors — fit for a prison!

Withdrawing money at the AIB bank in Tallaght. On the way out there was a bit of a queue due to the new doors they've installed. They're automatic and take a while to open. People were getting a bit annoyed with the slowness of the doors. One bloke in pure Dublin wit said,

'You'd get outta Mountjoy quicker than yed get outta heor!'

Overheard by Karl, Tallaght
Posted on Friday, 2 December 2005

## Spec Savers

At a wedding last Friday night and it was the best man's speech. He says, 'These are the loveliest bridesmaids I've ever seen, just gorgeous.'

Someone shouts out from the crowd, 'Ya should have gone to Spec Savers!'

Overheard by Vikki, at a wedding in Killiney
Posted on Monday, 28 November 2005

## So that's how the elite runners always win ...

Running the Dublin City Marathon a couple of weeks back. Running up the North Circular Road, which was closed to all road traffic while the marathon was going through, we went through a series of traffic lights (obviously redundant while the race was in progress) around Doyle's Corner. Smartarse behind me:

'Jaysus, I'd be winning if it weren't for all these feckin' red lights!'

Overheard by Gary, on the Marathon
Posted on Tuesday, 15 November 2005

# No age barrier

Overheard two elderly ladies on the no. 2 bus discussing the drug problem in Dublin:

Mary: 'Jaysus, Josie, aren't them drugs terrible?'

Josie: 'Mary, if it wasn't for the Valium, I'd be on drugs meself.'

Overheard by Mark, no. 2 bus

Posted on Saturday, 5 November 2005

# You don't have to go home but you can't stay here!

While in Slattery's pub in Rathmines for a few, I noticed a drunken old man hunched over the bar. As the evening went on he got more gargled and even more noisy! Eventually the barman told him to go home and helped him to the door. As he was leaving, he turned and told the barman politely to 'f**k off!' and that he had plenty of other pubs where he could go. Then he left.

All was quiet again for about five minutes when the old codger burst through the side door and stumbled up to the bar. The barman looks at him and says, 'I already told you to go home!'

The oul fella looks at him and while scratching his head in typical oul fogey fashion replies,

'Do you work in every f**kin pub in this town or wat?'

Overheard by Anonymous, Slattery's (Rathmines)

Posted on Thursday, 3 November 2005

# Who's the idiot?

Two students talking on the top deck of the no. 3 bus this morning. One, still drunk from the night before, sees a Garda directing traffic.

'Look at that idiot of a guard standing in the road wavin' at cars.'

Overheard by Busman, no. 3 bus
Posted on Tuesday, 1 November 2005

# I'm bleedin' crippled! But hey me appetite's good!

Was sitting in A&E in St James's Hospital and a doctor came to chat with the man on the trolley next to me. The doctor asked how he was and the man replied, 'I'm a bleedin' cripple, you let me out (of hospital) and now I'm a bleedin' cripple!'

The doctor could only tell him that he had signed himself out and he had been told not to walk on his legs. The man then proceeded to shout abuse and talk about filing a case. Then when the doctor asked how his wrist was, the man replied, 'Brand new, me wrist's fine.'

The doctor then asked how his appetite was, and the man replied, 'Me appetite's brand new, I love me appetite!'

Overheard by Daniel, St James's Hospital
Posted on Monday, 31 October 2005

## No rats allowed!

A corporation tenant complaining to a maintenance foreman, 'I have rats in my house!'

Without blinking the foreman replied, 'Ma'am do you not know it's against the bylaws to keep pets?'

Overheard by Gerry, complaints hatch in Council depot
Posted on Monday, 31 October 2005

## On the beat!

My friend, a trainee Ban Garda in Dublin, was called to a disturbance at a city centre pub. She encountered a drunken couple arguing. The following exchange took place after the husband pushed the wife:

Wife: 'Did you see that, you saw that, him pushing me an' all!'

Garda: 'Can we calm down a little and no I didn't see anything.'

Wife: 'Ye're all the f\*\*king same in your fancy f\*\*king uniforms, think yer're bloody brilliant, ya f\*\*king b\*\*ch!'

Husband: 'Don't take it out on her (pointing at the Garda's blue training badges), she's only bleeding training!'

Overheard by Jane, city centre pub
Posted on Sunday, 30 October 2005

## It's not unusual

On the DART — terrible Monday morning in bleakest winter, driver makes an announcement about something or other and the drones going into work pay no attention.

The next minute we hear the DART driver singing, with great gusto, 'My my my DE-LI-LAAAH, ahhhhh why why WHY! DE-LI-LAAAh!'

He had forgotten to turn his mike off … almost made going into work in a rain-storm feel OK.

Overheard by Joey, on the DART
Posted on Wednesday, 26 October 2005

## The old Blanch injury

A friend of mine was doing her nursing placement in A&E at James Connolly Hospital in Blanchardstown when a bloke was rushed in covered in blood. Immediately a doctor was called to the scene to inspect the West Dublin patient.

Doc: 'Can you hear me? Where are you bleeding from?'

Injured bloke: 'I'm bleedin' from Blanch …'

Overheard by Neill, James Connolly Hospital
Posted on Wednesday, 26 October 2005

## It's a wok not a pan!

In Lees Kitchen in Dalkey one Friday night, a guy was asking the Chinese guy behind the counter for ribs. Even though the shop was packed, he kept shouting that he wanted ribs, and every time the Chinese guy kept saying, 'No ribs!' With a growing crowd behind him, the guy does a HUGE fart. In the stunned silence that followed for a second, the guy says dead proud,

'Coooook dah in your pan!'

## Macker's house ...

I was on a plane over to London sitting in front of a youth soccer team. Just after the take off I overheard one of the young lads looking out the window saying,

'Here, Macker, I can see your house from here, I think it's on fire.'

## Any excuse for a pun!

Last Christmas, myself and pal buying our very first REAL Christmas trees for our respective new apartments. We were very excited and proud, and there before everyone else to get the pick of the bunch! After much deliberation we picked out two enormous trees, and as we struggled to get them to the check-out counter, dragging them behind us with difficulty but pride, we heard a broad Dublin accent shout from behind us:

'Jaysis, branchin' out are yis, girls?'

Overheard by Jess, B&Q, Liffey Valley
Posted on Thursday, 13 October 2005

## Eyes in me arse

Got on a no. 42 bus heading from Artane to the city. There was a newspaper on the seat and I was too lazy to move it so I sat on it. A fella gets on at the next stop and sits in the seat across from me:

'Are ya readin dat paper yur sittin on?'

Only in Dublin.

Overheard by Owen, no. 42 bus in Artane
Posted on Friday, 7 October 2005

## It's not just on Father Ted

Took my English husband to Dublin. Two lads were weaving down the road and one loudly said to the other, 'He has always been a fecking eejit!' My husband roared and said, 'They really do say fecking eejit over here!'

Overheard by Liz, O'Connell Street
Posted on Friday, 7 October 2005

## A smack of a lorry

Supermarket checkout. Little old lady buying 30 cans of cat food.

Old lady to checkout girl: 'I have three lovely cats. They are great company for me. I don't know where I would be without them.'

Checkout girl: 'Yeah. I had a cat once but he got a smack of a lorry and that was the end of that.'

Little old lady leaves hurriedly with her mouth still hanging open.

Overheard by ljr, Superquinn Sundrive

Posted on Thursday, 6 October 2005

## Loo-azz or Luas

Upon arrival at Heuston Station, having just stepped off the Limerick/Dublin train, I overheard a girl ask a lady where the Luas was.

'They're over there beside the men's Loo-aaz,' she replied, pointing at the ladies toilets.

Hmmm …

Overheard by brian, Heuston Station

Posted on Wednesday, 5 October 2005

## Say it slowly

In a restaurant with my kids, food arrives and my eldest girl (four years old at the time) says out loud something that sounds like, 'Where is my f\*\*king knife', to which my wife and I turn around in astonishment and stare at her.

'What did you say?' I ask in shock.

Slowly she says, 'Where is my FORK and knife?'

Overheard by stephen, in restaurant

Posted on Wednesday, 5 October 2005

# Soup anyone?

Was at Lansdowne Road for an Ireland game
recently, when a guy behind me shouted at one
of the soup-selling guys in the red boiler suits,
'Hey bud, have ya any soup left?' At that point
the guy turned around and said yeah, and
started to walk up towards the man. Then as the
terrace was silent he says,

'Serves ya right for making too much of it!'

Classic stuff!

Overheard by Darren, Lansdowne Road
Posted on Sunday, 2 October 2005

# Onions all wrapped up

Christmas Eve, 2004, small friendly supermarket
in Dalkey.

Struggling holiday temp on checkout: 'What do I
ring through the wrapping paper on?'

Exasperated colleague, clearly for the hundredth
time: 'Scallions!'

Overheard by maevesther, Dalkey
Posted on Saturday, 1 October 2005

# You tool ...

I'll set the scene. It's last period on a Friday
afternoon. We're doing Metalwork theory.
Everyone wishes they were somewhere else. The
teacher mentions the 'bastard file' and everyone
erupts into a fit of the giggles. After a five second
pause, the teacher says:

'Lads, there are many humorous phrases in

engineering: "bastard file", "bitch callipers".
Laugh now, and laugh hard, because by God you
have to get them out of your system.'

Overheard by Paulie, Metalwork class
Posted on Friday, 23 September 2005

## Contagious disease

Picture this. Swimming pool, south west Dublin.
All kids queuing up to have their showers after
swimming lessons, eagerly chatting away to each
other about their upcoming Holy Communion.

Tallaght girl asks quiet child beside her, 'When
are you making yer communion?'

Child answers: 'I can't, I'm Muslim.'

Tallaght child answers: 'Don't worry I had 'em
last week, you only break out in spots for a few
days, sure you'll be better in no time.'

Overheard by Margaret, Balrothery swimming pool, Tallaght
Posted on Tuesday, 20 September 2005

## Hope he spares her

I heard an old lady on a bus tell her friend, 'If
God spares me I'll be buried in Balbriggan.'

Overheard by Anonymous, on no. 19 bus
Posted on Thursday, 8 September 2005

## Honest Irish

I was standing outside a south Dublin pub with
random regulars. The lounge girl on duty came
out for a quick fag break. One elderly man

looked over towards her and said, 'You shouldn't be smoking, luv, it ruins your skin.' The girl nodded in agreement and smiled. The man spoke again: 'Ruin your skin you will and you have a lovely fat face.'

Overheard by Paddy, pub in Donnybrook
Posted on Tuesday, 6 September 2005

## Decent bus driver

I was getting off the bus one day and I thanked the bus driver as he was letting me off and he replies, 'It's alright, I was going this way anyway.'

Cheeky bastard.

Overheard by Kate, no. 48A bus
Posted on Tuesday, 30 August 2005

## Sauce

While queuing in McDonald's one afternoon I overheard the lad in front placing his order which went, 'Chicken nuggets an' a large coke, please.'

The girl behind the counter responded, 'What sauce would you like with the nuggets?'

'Ehhhh, what have you?'

The girl went on to list various dips. 'We have barbecue sauce, curry sauce, sweet and sour sauce, garlic mayonnaise ...'

To which the lad interrupted, 'Ehhhhh ... red.'

Overheard by J, McDonald's, Phibsboro
Posted on Tuesday, 30 August 2005

# How far is that?

Standing at a pedestrian light in the city centre I was queried by a confused looking American tourist who was pointing at the large real-time car park information board.

'How far is that?'

'Sorry?' I says.

Then he says a little more exasperated, wagging his digit at the sign again, 'Christ Church, 136 spaces — how far is that?'

Overheard by Derro, city centre
Posted on Monday, 29 August 2005

# More cinema exploits

Whilst watching the movie 'The Last of the Mohicans' in the Savoy many years ago. Daniel Day Lewis is just about to jump off the waterfall and turns to his girl and says, 'I will be back.' A young fella at the back of the cinema shouts: 'Good man Christie!'

The whole cinema exploded with laughter and the moment was ruined for the movie.

Overheard by Anonymous, Savoy
Posted on Monday, 29 August 2005

# Directions

One evening I was sitting on a bus going to Rathmines to meet a few friends. A few rows in front of me there were two Spanish girls who were a little flustered. One girl turns to a young lad sitting on the row opposite her and says,

'Excuse me, are you Irish?'

He replies, 'Yes.'

'Can you tell me where to get off the bus for Rathmines, please?' she asks.

Clueless, he answers, in a strong American accent, 'Sorry, I'm only half Irish!'

*Overheard by Legend, on a bus to Rathmines*
*Posted on Monday, 29 August 2005*

## Sometimes it's best just to smile and nod

While working in a heritage centre as a Viking re-enactor, an American tourist asked, 'Do you have reservations for your Vikings like we do for our Indians?'

Needless to say I was stumped.

*Overheard by Saoirse, Heritage Centre*
*Posted on Saturday, 27 August 2005*

## Quick cyclist

My sister was standing on the Canal bridge on Phibsboro Road, holding her shoe in her hand (the heel had come off). A young Dublin lad cycling along looked at her and without missing a beat says,

'Eh! Howiya Cinderella!'

*Overheard by Barry, Phibsboro*
*Posted on Friday, 26 August 2005*

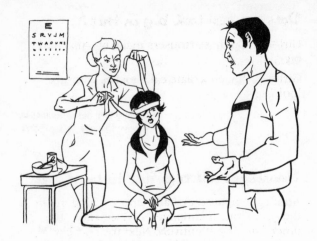

## Comic relief

Nurse bandaged up an anxious young woman's injured eye, assuring her it would heal completely, given rest. Her boyfriend broke the tension by asking,

'When does she get the parrot?'

Overheard by Sinéad, in the A&E department
of the Eye and Ear Hospital
Posted on Thursday, 25 August 2005

## Sedation

A mother talking to her young child who was running amuck in Topshop:

'Get off the floor for f**k's sake, you should of come with a sedative!'

Overheard by Jackie, Liffey Valley Shopping Centre
Posted on Thursday, 25 August 2005

# Does my bum look big in this?

Girl #1: 'Do these trousers make my arse look big?'

Girl #2: 'No, chocolate cake makes your arse look big!'

Overheard by Rob, on the Luas
Posted on Thursday, 25 August 2005

# Planning a robbery?

Noticed two 'head-de-balls' approaching me in the street, one in animated conversation, the other listening attentively. Next the speaker stops and puts down his Champion Sports bag, the better to describe something to his friend. All I could glean as I passed was,

'And dere's a gap of about dis much between de counter and de safe ...'

Overheard by Stephen, O'Connell Street
Posted on Wednesday, 24 August 2005

# The root cause of bad Irish weather

My Dad was in the barbers in Stillorgan a couple of months ago. He mentioned to the barber that the weather had been terrible recently. The barber replied,

'Must be all this globalisation.'

Overheard by Deirdre, barber shop in Stillorgan
Posted on Tuesday, 23 August 2005

# Wow! Window goes up, window goes down, window goes up, window ...

Couple of years ago on a rare sunny Irish day, two of my friends broke down in Glasnevin. Next thing a Garda car pulls up. Seeing as two young lads were driving a Range Rover, they were a bit suspicious.

Garda #1: 'What's goin on here, lads?'

Boy #1: 'We ran out of petrol.'

Garda #1: 'This your car?'

Boy #1: 'No, it's my mum's and yes, she knows I'm out in it.' Then the Garda starts walking around the car checking it out when he sees the back window.

Garda #1: 'What happened here, lads?' The two lads look a bit confused.

Garda #1: 'The back window. It's gone. What did ye do to it?'

Boy #1: 'Eh, nothing, it's electric.'

Garda #2: ?????? So one of the lads shows the Garda how the back window goes up and down.

Garda #1: (Shouts to Garda car) 'Jaysus, Paddy, get outta the car and look at this! Jaysus, lads, that's f**kin brilliant! Right, come on now and we'll get ye some petrol!'

Overheard by Ali, Glasnevin
Posted on Tuesday, 23 August 2005

# Long way around

I was listening to the 'Adrian Kennedy Phoneshow' one night and they were talking

about people who didn't ever want children.
One woman came on the show and said,

'I swear to God, Adrian, if I ever got pregnant I'd
swim the Atlantic Ocean to England to get rid of
it.'

Amazingly, no one pointed out to her what she'd
said!

Overheard by Emma, on the radio<br>Posted on Tuesday, 23 August 2005

## Hospital food

Was in a Dublin hospital in the early hours. A
drunk was sitting beside me. When he was
called to the counter, presumably the
nurse/receptionist asked him personal details
such as name, address, etc., to which he replied,

'Batter burger and chips, luv, I've been waiting
for f**king ages.'

Overheard by Michael, Mater Hospital<br>Posted on 23 August 2005

## Wife's hairdryer

I was in a Chinese take-away in Phibsboro after
the pubs closed. There were the usual drunken
racist remarks from a few lads in front of me.
Then one of them asked the Chinese man
behind the counter where he was from. The
man replied that he was from Hong Kong, to
which the other guy replied,

'That's a coincidence … my wife's hairdryer is
from Hong Kong!'

Overheard by Greg, Phibsboro<br>Posted on Tuesday, 23 August 2005

# Ice-cream, sir?

Whilst working in the ice-cream stall in Stephen's Green Shopping Centre, I was greeted by a rather plump man with a moustache, copious amounts of gold jewellery and a Dublin top.

Me: 'Ice-cream, sir?'

Dub: 'Yeah, cheers Bud, oide loike a plain one.'

Me: 'Vanilla?'

Dub: 'Did you not hear me or sumtin? I said I want a plain!'

I didn't stay too long in the job after that …

Overheard by James, St Stephen's Green
Posted on Tuesday, 23 August 2005

# O.J., OK

Little girl in Tesco in Mount Merrion.

Little girl: 'Daddy, can we get some O.J.?'

Daddy: 'We have plenty of O.J. at home.'

Little girl: 'Can we get "Apple" O.J.?'

Overheard by David, Tesco in Mount Merrion
Posted on Tuesday, 23 August 2005

# Vaccinate

A father and child came into a hospital emergency department and while giving details to the receptionist about the boy's dog bite the receptionist asked the father, 'Is he up to date with his vaccinations?'

The father replied, 'Jaysus, I don't know, I'll have to ring my next door neighbour.'

The receptionist asked, 'Why your neighbour?'

The father replied, 'Cos she owns the f\*\*king dog.'

Overheard by Paul, St James's Hospital
Posted on Monday, 22 August 2005

## Rules made in Ireland

I was in the bus station when I overheard a tourist enquiring about a bus that went to Limerick. She had got a timetable off the Internet that said the bus stopped in Kildare, her destination.

The helpful lady behind the enquiries desk said, 'Ah no, that's wrong, the Limerick bus only picks up passengers in Kildare and it does not drop off passengers.'

To which the tourist said, 'Run that by me again, it does a pick up but no drop off,' to which the reply was,

'That's right, but you could chance your arm with the driver and see if he'll drop you off.'

Overheard by Mary Maloney, Busaras
Posted on Sunday, 21 August 2005

## Clarification

I was on one of the no. 41s heading out to the airport (upper deck, bus was packed). A guy answers his phone and within seconds he begins a heated argument with the caller. It gets to the point where he's shouting, exclaiming that he is 'innocent', that he is 'not cheating' and he's 'on the bus out to Swords'.

He grows tired of his partner's accusations, jumps up out of his seat and turns to shout at the entire upper floor, 'My girlfriend on the other end thinks I'm cheating behind her back, everyone say hello!'

Everyone — 'HELLLOOOOO!'

He shouts back into the phone, 'Now are ya f**king happy!?' and hangs up.

Overheard by Martin, no. 41 bus
Posted on Sunday, 21 August 2005

## Irish film

I was in the UCI Coolock to see a film recently and when the censor's cert came on some young wan at the front says to her mates, 'Aw jaysus it's in bleedin Irish!'

Overheard by Kenny, UCI Coolock
Posted on Sunday, 21 August 2005

## 'WHERE IS HE?'

A couple of weeks ago, at an amateur panto, the guy on stage is doing the whole 'HE'S BEHIND YOU' bit. On asking the audience for the last time, 'WHERE IS HE?', a child of no more than seven shouts from the front row,

'He's behind you, ya f**kin b*ll*x!'

Overheard by Gill, Stillorgan
Posted on Sunday, 21 August 2005

# He obviously forgot where he was

Whilst travelling on the rush hour Luas line recently, a man's phone began to ring. Man answers loudly,

'Howaya Sharon … yea, yea, on the Luas now … what's for dinner this evening … lasagne … oh lovely … what time will I call over …I'll see you at 6 o'clock so … OK I'll see you later, Sweet Tits! … bye.'

Overheard by Sean, on the Luas
Posted on Sunday, 21 August 2005

# Pub grub

Around 1990, mid-afternoon in an old-fashioned bar off O'Connell Street. The owner resents drinkers asking for food, but provides pretty basic sandwiches under duress. An American visitor comes in and asks him for a glass of stout and something to eat. As the owner starts to pull the Guinness, he calls down to the barman at the other end of the (long) bar,

'Hey, Christy, will ye stop scratchin' yer arse there and make this man a sandwich!'

Overheard by Anonymous, the Something Inn
Posted on Sunday, 21 August 2005

# Chipper slash emergency

Myself and my wife were in town late Wednesday night and decided to pop into Leo Burdock's for a fish supper on the way home. We parked the car, and proceeded to head towards the chipper. On the way a guy, obviously after a few 'gargles',

came running past us in the opposite direction,
to which we took no notice. Having installed
ourselves in the queue, the same guy re-
appeared, duly re-took his place in the queue
just ahead of us, and said, 'Jaysus, tanks a
million, I had to pop off for a slash ...'

Overheard by Gav, Leo Burdock's

Posted on Sunday, 21 August 2005

## Water safety Dublin style

Travelling on the DART from Howth to Connolly
Station last winter one cloudy morning,
approaching Raheny it started to rain heavily
and the speed of the train caused the rain to
blow in through an open window.

Woman in seat nearby: 'Oh quick quick close the
window I am drowning!'

Male voice from down the carriage: 'Don't worry.
missus I'm a lifeguard.'

Overheard by Sean, on the DART

Posted on Saturday, 20 August 2005

## Leppers?

Shortly after the smoking ban was introduced
into Ireland, I was standing outside a pub having

a smoke when I overheard two aul' ones in conversation.

One said, 'Jaysus, this smoking ban is a pain in the arse.'

To which the other replied, 'I know, jaysus, we're like bleedin' leopards out here.'

## Paradoxical law enforcement

My brother and his girlfriend had pulled over in their car, when a guard came along and tapped on the window:

'If you want to stay here,' he said, 'you better move along.'

## Baileys sans Irish cream

Two middle-aged American ladies standing at the bar: 'Any idea what you are goin to have?'

'I'm getting the Baileys Irish Cream.'

'Mmmmm can you order one for me too … without the cream.'

## Not religious?

One day my boss (who is a know-it-all) and I were discussing the new bottle of cleaning fluid he'd bought and he asked me what I thought the smell reminded me of. I said white spirits or something like that and he said,

'Oh I know that smell, it's the same stuff they used in the hospital when my daughter was born, to clean her after they cut her UN BIBLICAL cord.'

Overheard by kc, work
Posted on Friday, 19 August 2005

## Euro changeover

When I was working in the Allsports café at the time of the euro changeover in Dublin, one of my colleagues had a unique way of asking customers if they wanted money changed from pounds to euro.

Customer arrives at the counter with Irish punts and he would ask,

'Would you like me to "euronate" that for you?'

Overheard by Julyan, Allsports café
Posted on Friday, 19 August 2005

## You've got to admire him

I was standin' outside Farringtons havin' a smoke when a taxi was just about to pull away from Fitzsimons. These two English chicks ran to catch it, hailing ...'TAXI! TAXI!' ... to which the driver lowered his window and roared ...'PASSENGER! PASSENGER!' ... and drove off!

Overheard by Red, Temple Bar
Posted on Thursday, 18 August 2005

## Never stop for a hoodie

Coming past Baker's Corner on the no. 46A, some kid in a hoodie broke into a run to catch the bus. The bus obligingly stopped, and the kid, instead of boarding, stands and asks, 'Are yeh goin' to Dun Laoghaire?' (As if this wasn't printed on the front, as if this wasn't a friggin' 46A coming back from town!)

The driver says yeah, and the kid says, 'That's great for you, Mister! Cause I'm not goin' there!' and runs off.

Overheard by Lee, no. 46A bus in Dun Laoghaire
Posted on Thursday, 18 August 2005

## Americans

I was sitting on the Luas at the Four Courts Luas stop. Two American women sitting beside me. Out the window I saw two elderly gents, obviously barristers, horsehair wigs, long black gowns, briefcases, the lot, walking into the courts. One of the Americans pipes up,

'Oh look, they must be graduating!'

Overheard by Robbie, on the Luas
Posted on Thursday, 18 August 2005

## Expensive service

In a café on Camden Street. Foreign couple walk in (obvious tourists — camera around neck, sandals with socks etc.) and ask the run-off-her-feet waitress, 'Can we smoke in here?', to which the girl replies,

'Of course you can but it will cost you a €3,000 service charge and you may or may not have to visit Mountjoy!'

The confused look on offending tourist's face was class!

Overheard by J, Café Sofia
Posted on Tuesday, 16 August 2005

## Where do you want to have it?

Lad in front of me ordering his food, cashier asks him, 'Are you having it here?' Lad looks around and points down at an empty table,

'Nah, I'll have it over there if that's alright.'

Overheard by Theo, Burger King Coolock
Posted on Tuesday, 16 August 2005

## A head fetish

Overheard on the no. 77A from town. Five excited kids get on at the Coombe.

'Come on! Upstairs, the front seat,' one of them shouts, 'We can look at the driver's head!'

Overheard by Johnner, The Coombe
Posted on Saturday, 13 August 2005

## Give the child a name!

My sister's friend had a baby boy a couple of weeks ago. After the birth everyone was sitting around discussing the new arrival. The child's grandmother asked the parents what name they were thinking of giving the child.

Mother: 'We're probably going to name him Marc with a "c".'

Grandmother: 'CARK?!'

Overheard by Dermot, Stillorgan
Posted on Thursday, 11 August 2005

## The look of the draw

On the no. 65B bus on the way home. Two 'howyas' talking rather loudly. One girl said to the other, 'I'm after gettin me house.' The other girl replies, 'Bout bleedin time.' The first girl then says, 'Yeah, but no side entrance.' The second girl goes,

'Give tha back, no side entrance, that's takin the piss, how ya supposed to get your wheelie bin out!?'

Overheard by Barbara, no. 65B bus
Posted on Wednesday, 10 August 2005

## The way to Amerilla

On the no. 19 bus the other day a young woman gets on with her 6-year-old daughter. After a while the little girl starts singing, 'Is this the way to Amerilo …' The mother decides to join in, 'Every night I've been huggin' my pilla.' To which the young girl replies in flatist Dub accent,

'Jaysus, Ma, it's not "pilla" it's "pillow", you're real common, d'ya know tha!'

Overheard by Jen, no. 19 bus
Posted on Monday, 8 August 2005

# Road rage?!

A taxi pulls out across the path of a car in traffic.
The car driver honks the horn at the taxi driver.
The taxi driver without batting an eyelid shouts
back at him,

'Ah, save yer horn for yer missus!'

Overheard by Ogmios, St Stephen's Green
Posted on Monday, 8 August 2005

# What would you like to watch?

Sitting in UGC cinema during the trailers, an
advertisement for Sky Movies came on, talking
about all the movies you can watch. At the end
the voice-over on the ad says, 'WHAT WOULD
YOU LIKE TO WATCH?' to which some little
head-the-ball in front of me shouts at the screen,

'The bleedin film for f**k sake!'

Overheard by Kyra, UGC Cinema
Posted on Monday, 8 August 2005

# Confession

One Saturday morning I was standing in a very
long queue in an electrical wholesalers. The
queue was out the door and literally following a
queuing system like that in the airport. Anyway,
this little old lady about 84 years joins the queue
behind me, sighs and says,

'Ah Jaysus! Only one priest on again.'

Overheard by Des, Dublin
Posted on Friday, 5 August 2005

# Lamest Luas joke ever!

While waiting at the Luas stop at the Red Cow roundabout the Luas approaches from a distance in its customary snail-pace like fashion. Two impatient guys start criticising the speed of the tram.

One of the guys: 'Jaysus! It's no Carl LEWIS.'

Overheard by Paul, Red Cow Luas stop
Posted on Friday, 5 August 2005

# Very affordable housing

I'm in the back of a car with my friends. The front-seat passenger is browsing through the property section of the *Irish Times*:

Driver: 'Did you read that about a fella buyin a parking space in an underground car park in town for 10 grand!?'

Front-seat passenger (thoughtfully): 'Cud ya build on it!?'

Overheard by Seany, in a car in Malahide
Posted on Thursday, 4 August 2005

# Paki surprise

I brought an English friend to a Dublin versus Meath match. He's from London but is of Indian origin. As we were leaving the match a bunch of Hill16ers were coming towards us singing, 'I'd rather be a Paki than a royal, I'd rather be a Paki than a royal', by coincidence.

I realised with horror what would happen but it was too late. As they passed my 'Indian' friend they saw him and started to rub his hair and throw their arms around him, singing louder.

As they passed us by all you could hear was one fan shouting, 'That was f**king great … we were singing about Pakis and then one arrived.'

Overheard, outside Croker by Shane
Posted on Wednesday, 3 August 2005

## Bring on the harassment lawsuit ...

Coming up to the counter in McDonald's, I heard the middle-aged manager say to the tired-looking girl sweeping the floor: 'Go on, sweep me off my feet.'

I had to bite my lip ...

Overheard by Anonymous, McDonald's, Blackrock
Posted on Wednesday, 3 August 2005

## The effort a Dub will go to ...

Travelling on the no. 79 bus from Ballyfermot into town, we got stuck in mad traffic along the quays. There were two young lads sitting a few seats in front of me on the upper deck. One of the lads looks out the window and spots someone they know walking on the footpath on the other side of the Liffey. He says aloud to his pal, 'Loook — it's bleedin' Anto.'

The lad jumps up on the seat and opens the window (the old slidey type) and for the next few minutes roars as loud as he can, 'ANTO, ANTO, AAAANNNTO!'

Finally, Anto hears them and looks over. To which he continues, 'YOU'RE ONLY A LITTLE BOLLIX!'

Overheard by Max, no. 79 bus

Posted on Wednesday, 3 August 2005

## Sorry, no exchanges or refunds

Going into the Coombe with my older sister, helping her carry her 2-month-old daughter who was asleep in one of those car seats with the handle, and this Dub who was outside having a smoke looks me in the eye and says,

'Ahh here bud, you can't give them back you know!'

Overheard by Mick, front steps of the Coombe Hospital

Posted on Wednesday, 3 August 2005

## Drink responsibly ...

Myself and a couple of friends were waiting for one of the buses in the centre of Dublin that were organised to take people going to the Oxegen music festival last month. There were Gardaí at the stops making sure the queues didn't get out of hand.

Anyway, everyone there seemed to be carrying crates of beer and such in the hope of smuggling them into the concert area, when this country lad carrying a huge crate of Dutch Gold turns around as he was entering one of the buses that had just arrived and shouts to one of the Guards (clearly happy he's able to flout the anti-public drinking laws),

'Hoi, Guard, just off to do some major binge drinkin', ya know yourself,' followed by a grin and a wink, and soon after followed by nasty frowns by all the Gardaí present.

Overheard by Jim, off O'Connell Street
Posted on Wednesday, 3 August 2005

## Beatle with curry sauce, please

After getting their curry off the local curry-shop owner, Ringo, nearly every oul' fella — full of gargle — says,

'Cheers, Ringo, you're a star!'

Overheard by Derek, most weekends in Ballyfermot
Posted on Wednesday, 3 August 2005

## Culture vultures

A while back, when the James Joyce bridge (the one down near Guinness) on the Liffey was only opened after about 200 years in the process, I was going by on the bus, half listening to the chitchat. Two oul' ones in front were admiring the bridge.

One says to the other: 'Isn't it gorgeous all the same. It's just like that bridge in Sydney ...'

Exactly like it, if you ask me.

Overheard by Derek, on the no. 79 bus on the quays
Posted on Wednesday, 3 August 2005

## A Dublin emergency

I work in a pharmacy and we get many strange incidents but this one tops them all. A 15-year-old lad comes running in one morning looking rushed and out of breath. So I'm thinking, emergency, first aid needed, or he needs an inhaler.

Runs up to counter: 'Do ya sell stationery?' I check to see if I heard him correctly: 'Em sorry this is a pharmacy.' To which he replies,

'Is there nowhere in this f\*\*kin city that sells a rooooler at noyen a clak in da mornin?!'

Overheard by John, at work on O'Connell Street
Posted on Tuesday, 2 August 2005

## Everyone has their breaking point

One day walking down our main thoroughfare past the bus-stops outside the BOI, the crowds were heavy. Some girl with a thick Dublin accent, of about 18 or 19, was waiting for her bus. People must have been brushing off her and bumping into her on their way past, for all of a sudden, from out of the general din of the crowd she shouted out to the anonymous pedestrians,

'The next person who bumps into me's gonna get a f\*\*kin diiig!'

Only in Dublin.

Overheard by Kevin, O'Connell Street
Posted on Monday, I August 2005

## The wrong road to Tallaght

On the Luas to Ranelagh, Friday night around 11. Guy who's totally off his head and mumbling general abuse to all the young ladies around him suddenly bursts out with a tuneless homage to John Denver:

'Country road! Take me home!

To the place where I go!

Tallafornia! [incomprehensible]

Country road, country road!'

Overheard by mojo, the Green Line Luas
(to Ranelagh, not Tallaght)
Posted on Saturday, 30 July 2005

## Howaya, Guard

Myself and three of my friends were sitting in my car, just having a laugh, listening to music. When out of nowhere two Gardaí appeared, one at each side of the car (obviously they thought we were up to something). I rolled down the driver window and the Garda said:

'Howaya lads, we're the Guards,' to which my friend could only reply,

'Howaya Guards, we're the lads!'

Overheard by Janey Mac, in my car
Posted on Friday, 29 July 2005

# Chicken wings

Guy: 'Do you have any chicken wings there love?'

Girl behind counter: 'Yes.'

Guy: 'Then fly over there and get us a burger will ya.'

Overheard by Mark, Super Macs, O'Connell Street
Posted on Friday, 29 July 2005

# Inspiring words

After finishing a match some years ago I decided to stick around to watch another. Standing on the sideline in amongst the locals the match was tight and coming up to the final whistle. One of the players 'Willie' was chasing his marker to win the ball. Cue an over-excited manager shouting at the top of his voice,

'GO ON WILLIE GET UP HIS ARSE!'

Both sidelines erupt into fits of laughter as the play continues on but the manager's face turns a very bright crimson after realising what he had said.

It was lost on some of the younger supporters ... just as well really.

Overheard by Deano, Malahide Castle
Posted on Thursday, 28 July 2005

# Bargain Town

Sitting on the no. 39 going into town, two brothers, guessing about seven or eight, hop on with their ma and sit down the back. One of them starts singing the 'bargain town' theme off the radio, 'Hurry on down to bargain town!' again and again. He had a pretty rough accent but strains to make 'town' sound like the radio, more and more each time.

The elder brother goes, 'Will ye shurrup! Yer wreckin' me head! It's "taown"!'

'Hurry on down to bargain town!'

'It's "taowin"!'

'Hurry on down to bargain town!'

'It's "taowin"!'

'Hurry on down to bargain town!'

'F**ksake, ma, will ya tell him, it's "taowin"!'

'Stop annoyin' yer brother. It's "taown".'

'Hurry on down to bargain town!'

Slap! Tears.

Overheard by Anonymous, sitting on the no. 39
bus going into town
Posted on Thursday, 28 July 2005

## There's always one

Back in '97 I was in the Ambassador cinema, as it was then, watching the film of the moment, 'Titanic'. We were at the scene where one of the lifeboats returns to the masses of floating bodies, searching for survivors. Everyone of course was very quiet and subdued at this poignant moment, holding their breath for a reply as the officer manning the boat called, 'Is anyone alive out there?'

A guy (real Dub!) up the balcony of the cinema just couldn't bear to leave this question unanswered, and so breaking the dead silence pipes up, 'Over here!' at the top of his lungs.

The whole place erupted! It certainly was worth sitting through the whole three hours for that — there's always one!

Overheard by Aoife, Ambassador Cinema
Posted on Thursday, 28 July 2005

## Knickers

In Dunnes Stores underwear department. My sister's boyfriend holds up a pair of knickers and shouts all over the shop,

'Hey, Nora, I see your knickers are coming down in the sale.'

Overheard by Robert, in Dunnes Stores underwear department
Posted on Thursday, 28 July 2005

## No love on the line

While queuing in the GPO, I was standing behind a very well dressed gentleman in a suit. The queue line was all over the place and a lady in an equally flamboyant dress pushed in, in front of him. The two started arguing and it almost came to fisticuffs.

In behind the fortified counter the An Post guy winks at me and starts singing and waving his arms above his head from side to side (à la John Lennon):

'And all we are saaaaaying, is give peace a chaaaaance ...'

Overheard by Big Gaz, GPO
Posted on Wednesday, 27 July 2005

# Fore!

I was sitting on the bus when it pulled up at a stop just outside a public golf course. The doors opened and two fellas threw the golf bags over their shoulders and climbed on to the bus.

'Didn't see it comin' in here lads,' said the driver.

Wasted behind a wheel, I thought to myself!

Overheard by Brian, lower deck of the no. 42 bus

Posted on Wednesday, 27 July 2005

# The innocence of a wee one

I was flying into Dublin a few weeks back and we were coming into land. There was pretty much silence on the plane as we were descending. Only the voice of an innocent, young child can be heard. Real excited:

'Yay, we're going to land. Yay, Mammy, we're going to land. Yay, we're going to land. Yay!' (That may not be verbatim, but you get the picture. A giddy child, excited about the plane landing.) Everyone around has a nice little smile, while listening to the happy child.

Just as we are about to hit the tarmac there was a few bounces and a slight struggle to keep control of the plane. Nothing too drastic, but enough for you to instinctively grab the back of the chair in front.

Next thing the same little child, now panicked, is squealing: 'No, Mammy, I don't like it. I've changed my mind. I don't like landing. I don't like. NO! I don't, it's not nice! AAarrrgggghhh!'

It probably was scaring the child, but all on the plane just burst out laughing ...

Overheard by Hungover Child, Ryanair flight coming into land in Dublin Airport
Posted on Tuesday, 26 July 2005

# Not from the barrel of a gun

I was waiting for a no. 34 bus in Church Street listening to two old biddies — a long time ago before all but three births per year were to single mothers.

'D'ya see the Foleys' youngest is after gettin married?'

'Gaway, tha was quick, was she pregnant or what?'

'Naa, don't think so.'

'Jayz, there's posh for ya.'

Overheard by Brian, Church Street bus stop
Posted on Monday, 25 July 2005

# Don't we all ...

Man in Eddie Rocket's restaurant at 3 a.m., holding on to the counter, intoxicated, proclaiming, 'I love eating, I love it. I love eating ...'

Overheard by Jim, Eddie Rocket's, Dame Street
Posted on Monday, 25 July 2005

## Maybe he was really hungry?

On the no. 49 bus going out of town the other night, a pissed aul fella (he had wicked eyebrows, but that's another story) gets on and sits across from a young lad. Nothing unusual till the old man leans over towards the young bloke and slurs,

'Here lad ... do you know the ingredients of soda bread?'

Overheard by GCW, on the no. 49 bus
Posted on Sunday, 24 July 2005

## A quite packed Luas ...

Packed sardine-can-like Luas, in the silence of it, one lad shouts out to whoever ... Tony it might have been,

'HEY TONY WHAT'S YOUR FAVOURITE HUMMING NOISE!'

The silent laughter around the Luas is brilliant!

Overheard by Bucky, on the Luas, Connolly Station line
Posted on Saturday, 23 July 2005

# Choo choo sardines

I decided to take an extremely crowded Luas tram to Connolly to head for Croke Park for the Dublin versus Wexford match. With the Luas packed to capacity, it pulled up to the Red Cow roundabout, doors opened, and with that some smart-arse shouts to the unsuspecting passengers on the platform,

'Come on, hop on the Bangladeshi express!'

Overheard by Ray, Luas tram
Posted on Friday, 22 July 2005

# What every culchie dreads hearing ...

On their way to the Leinster football final last Sunday, a bunch of lads in Laois jerseys were walking up Clonliffe Road, trailed by a bunch of lads in Dublin jerseys. The Dublin lads were messing around, taunting and jeering the 'culchies'.

A worried flush rose on the back of the Laois lads' necks when the Dubs started singing, 'We saw where you parked your car, doo-dah, doo-dah!'

Overheard by Flan, outside Croke Park
Posted on Friday, 22 July 2005

# Dublin barmen ... aren't they great!

Sitting in Mulligans pub on Poolbeg Street having a pint at the bar, when a Yank came up and said to the barman, 'Excuse me sir, where is your bathroom?'

So the barman gave him directions and off went the Yank. A few minutes later the Yank returns and says to the barman, 'Excuse me sir, there's no lock on the door.'

The barman replied without looking up from the pint of Guinness he was pulling, 'As long as I've been here, no one ever tried to rob a shite.'

Overheard by Butty, Mulligans pub

Posted on Friday, 22 July 2005

## Dublin Bus ... serving the ENTIRE community a piece of their mind!

A pleasant summer evening, on the lower deck of the no. 90 bus, which is about half full of locals/tourists/culchies.

We're coming up the quays from Heuston Station towards town when the driver slams on the brakes. The whole bus lurches to the right, as a car has driven across its path. Everyone is shocked/startled and silent at this.

The next thing we hear is the bus driver leaning out the window bellowing at the top of his lungs.

'F**KIN' foreigners!'

The whole bus, foreigners and all, erupted in laughter.

Overheard by John, on the no. 90 route to Connolly Station

Posted on Thursday, 21 July 2005

## THE LEGS!

One sunny afternoon in Phoenix Park a mate of mine had to relieve himself. He found a quiet spot and attended to nature. Moments later a muppet-mobile (you know the drill, six muppets crammed into an old Toyota Starlet) comes around the corner. The windows lower, standard head-the-ball sticks his head out and roars, 'Heeeere you … with THE LEGS!' and the mobile speeds off.

My mate (bewildered by this stage) stands there confirming, 'Yes, I have legs. Well spotted.'

Overheard by Leno, Phoenix Park
Posted on Thursday, 21 July 2005

# Jayo!

Was in the Temple Bar on Dorset Street after a Dublin match, when a Chinese fella in a Dublin jersey crossed the road in front of the jammed pub. With no prompting the whole pub started chanting 'Jayo, Jayo, Jayo' in unison. Obviously the Chinese fella was scarlet and turned a bright shade of red but still managed to raise his arm and acknowledge the crowd and everyone fell about laughing.

Class.

Overheard by D, Temple Bar, Dorset Street
Posted on Wednesday, 20 July 2005

# Someone didn't learn their spellings!

I was coming home from college last November, on the no. 65B. As I got upstairs I got a real strong smell of hash! I saw a group of 14-year-old skanger lads sitting at the back talking and smoking away! One lad walked up and said, 'I'm gonna write "JOINT" on the window,' as they were fogged up!

In true skanger style he wrote 'GIANT'. Nice to know that being high didn't affect his ability to spell!

Overheard by Stephen, over the M50, Tallaght
Posted on Tuesday, 19 July 2005

## Well, that's alright so!

I was down in the courts recently for work. We were waiting for our case to be heard and had to listen to several young lads who were up for drink driving, theft etc. There was this young lad in particular who stood out; he had smashed up a few cars in a rage and the following was his defence!

Judge: 'So, can you tell me why you smashed up the three cars?'

Lad: 'Coz some bleedin foreigner upset me girlfriend.'

Judge: 'What had that got to do with the owners of the three cars? What had they done to upset you?'

Lad: 'Well, yer man ran off so I couldn't get him.'

Judge: 'So you took it out on the owners of the cars?'

Lad: 'Well I was bleedin mad wasn't I?'

Judge: 'So you just lash out when you're angry?'

Lad: 'No, judge, I don't.'

Judge: 'But you just said you lashed out because you were mad.'

Lad: 'Yeah, but I don't usually.'

Judge: 'So why did you this time?'

Lad: 'Cause I was off me bleedin head wasn't I?'

Overheard by Nuls, in the Four Courts
Posted on Tuesday, 19 July 2005

# Fire safety

Our Fire Safety warden at work sent around a survey of what we would do in case of a fire.

One of the questions was, 'What steps would you take if you discovered a fire?'

Some witty so-and-so replied, 'Very big ones.'

Overheard by Andy K, the office
Posted on Monday, 18 July 2005

# Face paint issues

Drinking and dancing in Flannagans last Saturday night, I went to the toilet and there was lots of chatting and yapping going on like usually in the ladies. Then suddenly this chick comes out with,

'There is only one problem: I don't have my eyebrow pencil with me!'

The problems that can arise on a night out …

Overheard by Kim, Flannagans pub
Posted on Thursday, 14 July 2005

# How romantic …

Old guy in a printshop in Dundrum discussing the new receptionist:

'Jaysus, I'd crawl through a mile of glass just to throw stones at her shite.'

Overheard by Mark, Dundrum

Posted on Thursday, 14 July 2005

## Holy God!

At my yearly visit to church on Christmas Day. The family in front of me obviously weren't regular Mass-goers either, because when the priest came out onto the altar, the 4-year-old son turns to his mother and yells at the top of his voice,

'There's God! You're in big trouble now!'

Overheard by Anna, in church, Greenhills

Posted on Tuesday, 12 July 2005

## Go toilet in a shop???

When my sister was working in a sports shop, she heard a father with son.

Son: 'Da, I need to go toilet, will ye bring me?'

Father: 'Awh jaysus, just go behind dat rail der!'

Overheard by ashy, JD Sports in Liffey Valley

Posted on Saturday, 9 July 2005

## Druid man

A drunk with a can of Druids in his hand is chatting up the girls behind the counter. He's blabbing on for ages about how his wife won't get out of bed so he brought her raspberries. Mid-speech he looks closely at one of the girls' breasts and says, 'That's a lovely name!'

Girl peers down at her t-shirt for a minute, then bursts out laughing, 'That's not my name!'

'It is,' said the drunk, peering closer. 'Spar! Where are you from?'

Overheard by Nicola Cassidy, Spar shop on Camden Street

Posted on Thursday, 7 July 2005

## A child's logic!

Waiting in long queue to pay for car tax, at the back a young Dublin mother stands with her boisterous 10-year-old son. A Nigerian mother walks in the door dressed in full traditional dress and sandals. The 10-year-old yells up to his mother,

'Ma, that woman over there is black but why are her feet white?'

Overheard by Dermot, Car Tax Office

Posted on Wednesday, 6 July 2005

## Escaping exam questions

Three girls outside an O'Brien's Sandwich shop discussing exams. One says, 'I think my problem is that I don't read the question properly,' to which one of the others replies,

'Ooooh my God, that is like, so my problem too. I start answering the question, and then I go off on a tandem ...!'

One way of getting out of having to complete the exam!

Overheard by Daisy, O'Brien's Sandwich shop, D4

Posted on Wednesday, 6 July 2005

## Girlzandboyz

While unpacking shoe boxes in Dunnes Stores I overheard two women having an argument. After a few heated exchanges, one of them walked over to me and thrust a pair of kid's pyjamas under my nose and said,

'Here! Are dese for young wans or young fellahs?!'

Overheard by Nicola, Dunnes Stores, Ilac Centre, Dublin
Posted on Wednesday, 6 July 2005

## Who says chivalry is dead ...

Sitting upstairs on the no. 15A bus out of town. Passing through Rathgar, father and young daughter (five) make their way to stairs. Father is walking in front of little girl. Just as they reach the stairs, little girl screams, 'Ladies first!' Father steps aside ...

Chivalry is alive and well!

Overheard by Chuckster, on no. 15A bus
Posted on Tuesday, 5 July 2005

## Ask a stupid question ... in Dublin

In Grogans pub I overhead the following:

Bloke: 'Do yis have a toilet?'

Barman: 'What do you think?'

Barman (after bloke walks off): 'F**kin eejit.'

Overheard by old man, Grogans pub
Posted on Monday, 4 July 2005

## Mind the jacket

Shopping in Dunnes Stores in Crumlin a 2-year-old boy toddler was being chased by his 6-year-old sister. The girl proceeds to knock her brother down onto the floor and stomps her feet heavily onto his back, resulting in the child wailing. As I stared in disbelief their father appears.

'Ah, stop that now,' he says to his daughter, 'Ya'll ruin his good jacket!'

Overheard by Grainne, Dunnes Stores
Posted on Friday, 3 June 2005

## Just like heaven

On a Ryanair flight to Paris, just as we got above the white, fluffy clouds and it felt like we were walking on them, I heard a little Irish kid's voice squeak matter-of-factly above the din, 'Oh look, we're in heaven!'

Overheard by Alison, Ryanair flight to Paris
Posted on Saturday, 2 July 2005

## Funny butcher

Was in a butchers the other day and this girl walks in and says to the fella behind the counter, 'A pound a fillet.'

The fella turns around and says, 'A pound I don't!'

Overheard by Brian, Keoghs butchers in Crumlin
Posted on Saturday, 2 July 2005

## Who's Judas?

Was on a no. 10 bus in Dublin last Easter when I overheard these two Dubs in their twenties, going on about all that happened from Holy Thursday till Easter Sunday back in biblical times.

Judas came up in the conversation, to which one of the girls says, 'Judas?' And the other one went, 'Ya, Judas, ya know, yer man dat ratted on Jesus!'

Overheard by Jonathan, on a bus
Posted on Friday, 1 July 2005

## Tea and sambos

I was waiting for the Nitelink on Westmoreland Street a few years ago with a few mates and an oul lad came up to us and said, 'Ah jaysus lads can you spare us a pound for a cuppa tea and a sambo?'

Quick as a flash my mate said, 'Feckin' hell, a pound for a cup a tea and a sandwich! I want to know where you're going.'

Overheard by Pete, Westmoreland Street
Posted on Friday, 1 July 2005

# Ryanair and its quality staff

While on a Ryanair flight home from Gatwick the plane was on its way to the runway for take off and one of the air hostesses comes over the intercom:

'Cabin crew to landing position,' ... two seconds later ... 'or take off even!'

Overheard by Deano, London Gatwick
Posted on Thursday, 30 June 2005

# Italian stallion

On a packed bus seated second seat from the back upstairs, when a group of school kids start having a conversation about religion.

One of them goes, 'I'm a Catolic!'

Another one goes, 'I'm a Roman Catolic.'

To which another one goes, 'Ya Italian bastard!'

Only in Dublin!

Overheard by Deavo, no. 16A bus
Posted on Thursday, 30 June 2005

# Giving account of yourself

A friend told me of an incident that happened to him recently. He was standing in the queue at the Credit Union. When he was almost at the top of the queue, with only one man in front of him, the loudspeaker announced: 'Counter number nine, please.'

The man in front of him did not move. My friend leaned over towards him to indicate to him that it was his turn when he heard the man whispering, 'One, two, three, four ...'

It then dawned on my friend that the man had interpreted the announcement as, 'Count to number nine please'!

Overheard by FJ Murray, Drimnagh
Posted on Thursday, 30 June 2005

# Inflation

I went down to Croke Park early before the last U2 concert to see if I could get a ticket. I came across a head-the-ball who was asking, 'Anyone buying or selling a ticket?'

I asked, 'How much are you selling them for?'

He replied, '250.'

I wasn't interested. However a young Asian tourist eagerly approaches the guy and asks, 'You have ticket? How much?'

Head-the-ball (while making sheepish eye contact with me): '300.'

The Asian guy willingly accepts.

Overheard by Paul, outside Croke Park
Posted on Tuesday, 28 June 2005

# Revealing graffiti

Some brilliant graffiti I saw on my way to work one morning and it still cracks me up to this day:

'Willo Murphy does the sunbeds.'

Overheard by Mel, Coolock
Posted on Monday, 27 June 2005

# Rashers

In a butchers in town a girl asked for a pound of rashers. The butcher asked her what type of rashers. The girl replies, 'The ones that you fry!'

Overheard by Ms Silly, butchers in town
Posted on Monday, 27 June 2005

# Love is not blind!

Coming out of the U2 concert on Saturday night, there were lots of women going ga-ga over the Garda horses. One girl says, 'Aaaah look at the horse, isn't it beautiful?'

To which her boyfriend replies, 'Well it's better looking than you!'

Overheard by Neil, outside Croke Park after U2 concert
Posted on Monday, 27 June 2005

# Tis not Russia you're in now boy ...

While waiting patiently to ask a member of the Garda Síochána directions to get to the Canal End, an English gentleman had approached him also looking for directions. Here is how the conversation went:

English guy: 'Hi mate can you tell me which way I go to get to the Kossack Stand?'

Guard staring blankly for a minute, but couldn't help himself: 'Tis not Russia you're in now, boy, keep going down there and it's on the right-hand side.'

Meanwhile I stepped up to ask my question, and I was trying to keep a very straight face, when the Guard said, 'I suppose you're looking for the Hoggan Stand.'

A Guard with a sense of humour, who would have thought it …

Overheard by Nicola, U2 concert
Posted on Monday, 27 June 2005

## Big knockers

One day in an Economics lecture we were all dozing off until this one-liner promptly awoke us. As our lecturer explained the natural ups and downs of an economy, he says,

'Lads, there is always going to be big knockers in society.'

As we all struggled to keep the laughter in, it must have clicked with him what he had said, so he told us to get it out and have a good laugh, to which we obliged! We didn't realise he was being sarcastic and told us all to shut up and stop being so immature.

Overheard by Laura, UCD
Posted on Friday, 24 June 2005

# Sun or sunbeds?

While in the changing rooms in Penneys in Rathfarnham I overheard two women who were trying on three-quarter length pants.

One said to the other: 'Mary would you not try on a pair of shorts, you'd get a lovely tan in the sun in Spain?'

To which Mary replied: 'Ah no, sure I wouldn't be bothered with the sun, I'll just do the sun beds when I get back!'

Wonders never cease!

Overheard by Eithne, Penneys in Rathfarnham
Posted on Friday, 24 June 2005

# Internet difficulties

This happened in a BESS lecture, perhaps proving that the lecturers are just as dumb as the students doing the course ...

While explaining the different ways to contact her if there were any problems, the lecturer has greatly endorsed using the Internet. Then she came out with,

'However, if any of you have trouble using computers or the Internet, please email me and we'll arrange a time to sort it out.'

Hmmm, didn't think that one through, did she?

Overheard by Boxty, in a Trinity lecture theatre
Posted on Thursday, 23 June 2005

# A Spaniard's farewell to Ireland

Just before departing on a flight to Madrid, a young Spanish student sitting behind us made a last-minute call. It went something like this (you'll have to imagine the Spanish accent):

'Hello, Eileen. I am on the plane and we are just about to leave. I have something to say to you, Eileen. This is very important to me. F\*\*k off, Eileen.'

And she hangs up.

Overheard by Dave, on flight EI 594
Posted on Thursday, 23 June 2005

# Is Marley Park outdoors?

Going to the Coldplay concert last night at Marley Park, in the pub before the gig with my girlfriend. I was looking out the window at the sun shining and said, 'This is some day for the gig.'

She replies, 'Is Marley Park outdoors?'

Should I keep seeing this girl …

Overheard by Mac, Temple Bar
Posted on Thursday, 23 June 2005

# Ask a stupid question …

Young lad in court for minor offence. Judge asks him, 'Are you working at the moment? Lad replies, 'Yes.' Judge asks, 'Who do you support?' Lad answers, 'Man Utd.' Judge, not amused, says, 'WHO do you support at home?'

'Oh you mean me Ma?!' came the reply.

Overheard by Bab, courthouse in Kilmainham
Posted on Wednesday, 22 June 2005

## Explaining the rules

In Quinn's, during Longford-Dublin match. Guy is explaining the concept of hurling and football to his girlfriend (who *is* Irish!).

Guy: 'If it goes between the posts and below the bar it's a goal, and that's worth three points; and if it goes between the posts and over the bar, that's a point.'

Girl: 'O right, yea, and what's a try …?'

Overheard by Edel, Quinn's Drumcondra
Posted on Wednesday, 22 June 2005

## Horse for sale

I was sitting on the no. 39 bus with a friend on our way home from town, talking to these lads who just decided to strike up a conversation. Just as we come to the dual carriageway a couple of head-the-balls get on and sit down beside us (we were sitting at the back) and started talking to the lads we had been making small talk with. When one of the lads, only about 12, turns around and says, 'D'ye wanna buy a horse?'

One of the lads turns around and says, 'What would I bleedin want with a horse?'

Another one of the lads decides to amuse the little lad and says, 'How much are ye sellin yer horse for?'

To all our shock and amusement the little lad turns to him and says, 'Well I don't know, I havta f**kin rob him first, don't I?'

Amazing!

Overheard by Tanya, on the no. 39 bus
Posted on Tuesday, 21 June 2005

## Women drivers

On a flight from Liverpool to Dublin on Aer Lingus, the pilot came on to give the usual pre-flight chat. Turns out it was a female pilot, much to the amusement of a group of middle-aged Dubs sitting at the back of the plane! Cheers went up, like 'Go wan ya good thing!' etc.

Anyway, the flight was relatively uneventful, but the landing was particularly bumpy. After bouncing off the tarmac about three times and finally shuddering to a halt, the pilot came on and apologised for the bumpy landing.

With that, one of the lads at the back shouts up, 'Ah jaysis, missus, I'd hate ta see yer bleedin parallel parkin!'

Overheard by Barry, Aer Lingus flight
Posted on Tuesday, 21 June 2005

# Duvets

One evening waiting for a friend outside Clery's, a group of three middle-aged, fake-tanned, make-up-caked-onto-their-faces women walk past. As they pass the Clery's entrance, one of them goes,

'Oh hang on Mary, I'll come to Ann Summer's with ya but I want to have a look at duvets in Clery's first.'

Bet she's a real tiger in the bedroom ...

Overheard by Squiggles, O'Connell Street
Posted on Monday, 20 June 2005

# Team worker

About a year ago a young lad started work in the office I work in, let's call him John. John and I were in different departments, however due to a shortage of desks he sat at the desk beside mine for the first two or three days.

John spent those first days asking me questions about what he should be doing etc. and I spent those first days responding that I was sorry but I worked in another department and could not help him, he should ask someone in his department.

A couple of weeks later at a staff night out, John, about a dozen co-workers and I were sat around a table. I asked John, 'So how are you getting on? All settled in?'

John eagerly answered, 'Oh, yeah thanks. The first few days I was sitting beside a right bitch, but I like where I am now.'

I never saw so many people decide to go get a round at the same time!

Overheard by Teresa, work night out
Posted on Thursday, 16 June 2005

## It pays to think before you speak, especially after watching Sky news!

My grandson was being christened in a church in Lucan. His name is Sam Adam. The priest held him up to the congregation and said,

'We would like to welcome Saddam into our church.'

The church rattled with laughter, as the red faced priest made the correction.

Overheard by Anonymous, St Mary's Church, Lucan
Posted on Saturday, 11 June 2005

## Two accents?

Some schoolgirl on her mobile on the Luas:

'Outside the school? Yeah I'm on the Luas, I'll be two minutes like. Yeah I'll be there. I'm fookin comin alrigh?! Will ya hold on ...Yeah, outside the school. Will ya fookin hold on! I'm comin! Jaysus! Fookin givin' me hassle.'

She gets off the phone to whoever it was and makes another call (in a blatant southside accent):

'Hello, yes, yes, I'm on my way. OK, excellent. Alroysh, heh, see you then.'

Overheard by Rob Gallagher, on the Luas between Charlemont and Windy Arbour stops
Posted on Friday, 10 June 2005

## Sober munch

My mate was on the DART last Holy Thursday
having a good snigger at some 'rock boys'
talking about how wasted they were going to get
that night. When one of them mentioned that
the pub would be closed tomorrow the other
said in disbelief,

'No way! Does that mean that loike Abrakebabra
will close as well?'

When the others said, 'No, why do you ask?' he
replied,

'Cos loike no one would eat that food sober.'

Overheard by claire b
Posted on Wednesday, 8 June 2005

## 'Car minding'

Up for a game at Croke Park a few weeks back.
Paid the €10 to the local 12-year-old 'head-the-
ball'-to-be so he'd look after the car. A BMW
parked behind and the young lad roars, 'Giz
€10 an' I'll mind yer car.'

Yer man replied, pleased as punch, 'No, that's
OK. I'm leaving my dog in the car. He's a
German shepherd.'

Without blinking the young entrepreneur
replies, 'Yea, sound. Here, can your dog put out
fires?'

Savage!

Overheard by Barry, Croke Park
Posted on Wednesday, 8 June 2005

## The very confident salesman

While relaxing on the Boardwalk along the Liffey on a sunny June bank holiday afternoon, my attention was drawn to a few animated head-the-balls who stopped nearby. One of them was taking packets of rashers out of an Elvery's sports shop plastic bag. He took out two packets at a time. For each time he took out a pair he declared,

'5', '10', '15', '20' etc., up to '50'.

I couldn't make sense of his mathematics. Why was he adding '5' for every two packets he pulled out? Then when he was finished he put all the packets of rashers back in the bag and headed off enthusiastically with his two mates, exclaiming,

'Sorted! That's €50 worth we have there — two packets for €5.'

A bargain!

Overheard by Pearse, Boardwalk at Eden Quay
Posted on Tuesday, 7 June 2005

## Where are the animals?

On a recent visit to a packed Dublin Zoo, we had an hour-long queue before we got in. Because it was the afternoon after the animal feeding time, all the animals were panned out in long grass and hence, out of sight. It was increasingly frustrating for the paying public.

One old couple I saw summed it up. The old man approached the window of the lion cage, had a quick look, threw his eyes up to heaven and walked on. His wife, just behind him asks,

'Anything in there, Charlie?'

Charlie replies sarcastically, 'Yeah, more f\*\*kin straw!'

Overheard by Anonymous, Dublin Zoo
Posted on Tuesday, 7 June 2005

## That's all they asked

British tourist: 'Do you know which side of the Liffey we are on?'

Dub: 'Yeah.'

Overheard by Aspro, Tara Street DART station
Posted on Monday, 6 June 2005

## Spot on

A friend was working in a Finglas Spar when two aul' ones came in, catching up with each other's weekend.

'We got a new video player and watched a few films.'

'Jaysis, that's great! What make is it?'

'Christ! I forget ... it begins with a "P".'

'Is it a Mitsubishi?'

'That's it!'

Overheard by PoC, Finglas
Posted on Tuesday, 7 June 2005

## Better value

An irate Dublin bus driver, roaring out the window at a bad driver:

'WHERE D'YA GET YER LICENCE? Tesco? Or
Dunnes Stores?'

Overheard by Mark, Portobello Bridge
Posted on Friday, 3 June 2005

## Lassies in danger

While walking up North Great George's Street I
noticed that the movie 'Lassie' was being shot.

There were Guards, directors, loads of actors in
old-fashioned clothes and of course the dog
Lassie. There were actually two Lassies —
probably just in case something happened to the
other one.

They were in their kennels in a white van and
the door was open so you could see both of
them. The van was surrounded by a group of
skangers who were trying to pet the dogs and
take pictures of them with their camera phones,
while they had a fag in their hands.

The two American women sitting in the front of
the van noticed what was happening after a
while. The one in the passenger side said, 'Em,
excuse me, sir, please don't do that, please leave
the dogs alone,' in her high-pitched American
accent.

The skanger replied, 'OK, OK, missuz, iym only
tryin to av a look a' dem.'

Then the woman said, 'OK, sir, you can look but
please do not put your hands anywhere near
them!'

'Alri!' he replies. After this the skanger repeated
what he had done, filling the back of the van
with smoke. The woman in the driver's seat got
out and slammed the door shut and once again

told him that he was told not to do that and he replied, 'OK, I'm sorry, I'm sorry, I wos only tryin to see de lovely little doggie.'

Overheard by Mr.b, North Great George's Street
Posted on Wednesday, 1 June 2005

## Clairvoyant auld ones

On the bus to Finglas yesterday an auld one got on and immediately spotted another auld one in front of me and they carried on with their greetings of 'Oh I haven't seen you in ages'. The conversation went from grandkids to health to the 'good old days'.

Auld one #1 says, 'Do you remember Mrs Kelly down the street who died in 1953?'

'Oh I do,' replies auld one #2, 'I went up to the house to see her laid out but sure I didn't know her till AFTER she was dead!'

Auld one #1 just said, 'Oh, that's a pity, she was a lovely woman!'

Overheard by Jennifer, no. 40C bus
Posted on Wednesday, 1 June 2005

## Apathetic response

I used to work part-time in Atlantic Homecare in Blanchardstown Centre as a shelf technician. One day, while stacking paint, I was asked a question that anyone who has worked in these kinds of service jobs is familiar with: 'Excuse me, luv, but do you work here?'

Having heard the question for the thousandth time that week, I lost interest in saying yes I do and replied, 'Oh sorry, I'm just wearing the official Atlantic Homecare replica jersey,' and walked off, leaving the woman apologising in my wake.

Overheard by NM, Atlantic Homecare
Posted on Wednesday, 1 June 2005

## Sex and the city ... hardly!

Three classy birds ordering cocktails last Friday evening in the Vaults. After much debating, they decided to go with cosmopolitans. They ordered from the rather stressed looking barman who proceeded to line up the glasses on the bar. The good looking blonde one said to her friend, 'Jaysus, there's loads of ice in them glasses, sure he won't fit any gargle into them.'

Her friend (from Cork I think) then said, 'Someone should say it to him that we don't want all that ice.'

She shouldn't have opened her mouth as her friends jostled her up to the bar and forced her to say it to him. She over-the-top politely called the barman over, apologised 17 times and asked him if he could take some ice out of the glasses.

The barman looked at her with disdain and disgust and replied, 'I'm cooling the glasses.'

Mortified Cork lass or wha!

Overheard by Reyo, Vaults Bar, IFSC
Posted on Wednesday, 1 June 2005

## Toto the chip man

The scene: An Italian-run chipper throbbing with people before a Dublin match in Croke Park.

One Dub (fresh out of the boozer after a morning's drinking) barely squeezes in the door and is at the back of a very long line. Not content with being at the back of the queue he starts to shout his order at the overrun Italian employees:

'BATTER BURGER AND CHIPS PLEASE.'

Clearly he is wasting his time so he tries a different angle to try and get their attention, so he shouts:

'HERE, SCHILLACI, GET ME A BLEEDIN BATTER BURGER WILL YA.'

Cue thunderous laughter from the rest of the line …

Overheard by Darren, Italian chipper in Ballybough
Posted on Wednesday, 1 June 2005

## Ramadanmalent

Two guys working behind the counter in Spar, one Dub, and one Asian. The Asian guy, apparently a Muslim, was explaining to his colleague about fasting during the holy month of Ramadan.

After hearing about this, the Dub declares, 'Yeah, sure we have that here too, only it's called Lent.'

Overheard by MP, Spar beside Pearse Street Station
Posted on Monday, 30 May 2005

## Just a normal day in Dublin so?

I was walking by the Ambassador on Parnell Street. Some old bloke was outside having a smoke and just shouts out,

'F\*\*king Sunday bloody Sunday and it's a f\*\*king Tuesday!'

Overheard by talkinghead, Parnell Street

Posted on Friday, 27 May 2005

## Queue for the no. 39 bus

There was a fire drill today at the Department of Health. There were about 300 people spilling out onto the street. One of the bus inspectors standing there yells,

'I hope you're not all for the bleedin' 39!'

Overheard by Anon, Hawkins Street

Posted on Wednesday, 25 May 2005

## Magic

Working in a very nice Dublin hotel in the carvery, when a little old dear comes up to the carvery chef and asks him if she can have the chicken soup but without too much chicken in it. Quick as a flash and totally straight faced he replies,

'Listen love, this is a chef's uniform not a magician's.'

Overheard by Dave, at work
Posted on Monday, 23 May 2005

## Not all it's cracked up to be

Last week on the bus passing the old Dundrum Shopping Centre, these two skangers sitting across from me look out the window and exclaim,

'Wouja lookit de new Dundrum Shoppin' Centre, bleedin' state of it already.'

Overheard by gdog, no. 63 bus
Posted on Saturday, 21 May 2005

## Dangers of running with child

I was strolling through Stephen's Green three weeks ago. Nice sunny day and everyone was in good form. Even the down and outs with their cans were smiling. Then this heavily pregnant woman came dashing by in a mad hurry. One of the beer-can wielding lads shouted,

'Don't run missus. You'll boil yer waters.'

Even the ducks were laughing.

Overheard by Paul Quinlan, St Stephen's Green
Posted on Friday, 20 May 2005

## Charity begins at home

In a charity shop a black man was buying a few items of clothing and a pair of flip-floppy type shoes. I don't know whether he didn't have enough to pay for everything or he was just chancing his arm, but he was asking for a discount on his combined purchases. The little old dear behind the counter was politely trying to explain to him that it's a bit cheeky to ask for discounts in a charity shop as the money goes to a good cause.

'I'm sorry dear, I can't give them to you for less, it's for charity, we're Gorta, the money goes to the third world, we help them out over there.'

To which he replied, 'The third world? Africa?!? That's me, help ME out over HERE!'

Overheard by Fenster, Gorta shop on Liffey Street
Posted on Friday, 20 May 2005

## Sounds a bit fishy?

I was walking down Moore Street a few years ago, past all the traders with their stalls of haddock, potatoes and bananas, when I heard a loud female voice calling in pure Dublinese:

'Maria, get that young wan off deh fish, she's no knickers on!'

Overheard by Alonzo, Moore Street
Posted on Thursday, 19 May 2005

## Urgent need of graffiti school

More overseen than overheard. Scribbled on the wall of the Four Courts some years back:

# House of Diseption

Overheard by Ug, Four Courts
Posted on Thursday, 19 May 2005

## Like he meant it!

Was walking down Grafton Street on my way to my exam the other morning. Little girl of about five was skipping towards me with her father behind her. She was generally laughing and giggling until she stopped in front of the window of La Senza lingerie shop. She looked at the mannequins and turned to her dad saying,

'Eeeeuuuuuw! Gross! Dad, look! Women's bottoms!'

Her father turned around like a shot, mouth hanging open, then caught himself and said, 'Yeah, ugh, really gross!'

Overheard by Sally, Grafton Street
Posted on Wednesday, 18 May 2005

## Elephants aren't what they used to be

Coming out of the UGC cinema on Parnell a while ago, and a group of guys who had just seen 'Alexander' were having the following conversation:

Guy #1: 'Did you see the way they had those elephants in the battle scenes, stomping on everyone?'

Guy #2: 'Yeah, it just goes to show you how strong elephants used to be.'

Overheard by gdog, UGC cinema, Parnell Street
Posted on Wednesday, 18 May 2005

# Irish racism

My brother was in a bike shop when a Chinese man entered the shop and asked one of the assistants for a tyre tube for his bike. The assistant asked what size tube he needed. The Chinese man said that any size would do.

When the assistant insisted that he couldn't sell him a tube unless he knew what size was needed, the Chinese man got agitated and said, 'You're being racist!'

At this point, another assistant in the shop piped up, 'How is he being racist? Sure you're not even black!'

Overheard by David, in a bicycle shop in town
Posted on Wednesday, 18 May 2005

# Outer magnolia

While shopping in Texas Homecare in Nutgrove, I overheard a woman ask her husband to reach up and pass her down a tin of MONGOLIA paint!

Call it a hunch but I think she may have meant Magnolia!

Overheard by John, Texas Homecare, Nutgrove
Posted on Tuesday, 17 May 2005

# Monkey magic

I was taking part in a college video last year. One scene involved a classmate climbing to the top of a 30-foot-high lamppost. Back in the editing suite we were looking over the footage when suddenly unknown to us this oul fella walks into the background of the shot and says as clear as a bell,

'Jaysus, someone should giv' 'im a ban-nan-na.'

Overheard by Martin, Ballyfermot
Posted on Monday, 16 May 2005

## Silly sausage

Was in the queue at a hot-food counter recently and the guy in front of me was asking the girl behind the counter for a sausage roll. The girl asked if he'd like a large sausage roll or a small sausage roll.

'No, a SAUSAGE ROLL,' says the guy.

'OK, a large one then is it?' the girl asks, pointing to the sausage rolls on display. To which she gets screamed back at her,

'Are ye f\*\*kin' steupit, a ROLL wit some SAUSAGES in it …'

Overheard by Noxy, shop in Dublin
Posted on Monday, 16 May 2005

## Whole finger …?

Overheard two blokes I work with in Swords one day in the locker room:

Bloke #1: 'Did ya hear about Danny's accident at the weekend?'

Bloke #2: 'No, wha happened?'

Bloke #1: 'Got his hand caught in one of the pressing machine rotors.'

Bloke #2: 'Jaaayyssisss, was he badly hurted?'

Bloke #1: 'Got one of his fingers really bad and ripped it off!'

Bloke #2: 'Jaaayyssisss ... the whole finger?'

Bloke #1 (deadly serious): 'No ... the one beside it.'

Overheard by Alan, work place in Swords
Posted on Monday, 16 May 2005

## Jews and their smokes

Just around when the smoking ban came in there was a phone-in show on the radio about it, and this one guy (Anto) rings in giving out.

Anto: 'Aaah ya knoo I just think da smokin ban is ya kno simetic ...'

Radio Guy: 'Wha?'

Anto: 'Aaah no ya kno anti simetic.'

Radio Guy: 'The smokin ban is anti Jewish?'

Anto: 'Aah well ah ...'

Overheard by Tomo, FM 104
Posted on Monday, 16 May 2005

## Tightrope act

While walking through St Stephen's Green I stopped to watch this lad walking the tightrope and playing the fiddle at the same time. There were two lads in front of me and one says to the other,

'Sure that's bleedin useless, he's not even blindfolded.'

Overheard by Anonymous, St Stephen's Green
Posted on Sunday, 15 May 2005

## Good old northsiders

I was at the bar one day and I overheard two lads ordering their drinks:

'Here mister give us a pint of Bulmer and I'll ave a pint of Millers.'

Smart-arse barman says to a co-worker:

'John, go out there and take the 's' off the Bulmers and put it on the Miller!

Overheard by tom, pub on the northside
Posted on Saturday, 14 May 2005

## Seals Rising from the Dead

A teacher was talking about the Irish Seal Sanctuary; he started telling us about an autopsy and what was involved in it. At this point one of the lads in the class put up his hand and said,

'Was he alright afterwards?"

Overheard by The Cheese, a classroom in Dublin
Posted on Saturday, 14 May 2005

## Cakin'

Two girls are about to enter a classroom on a hot day. One turns to the other:

'Ah no, I'm goin' t' be bleedin' bakin' in here!'

The other laughs and retorts, 'What are yeh? A bleedin' cake?'

Overheard by Dave, Swords
Posted on Friday, 13 May 2005

## Best chat up line ever

Was walking along the road the other night when a car drives by with a few lads in it and all I hear is,

'You're luvly ya are! I'd do 10 years in Mountjoy for ya!'

Overheard by Lisa, Stillorgan
Posted on Thursday, 12 May 2005

## The Irish culinary appreciation society

I was working in the restaurant one day when two girls came in and ordered two sandwiches from the menu. It states on the menu that all of the hamburgers and sandwiches are served with side salad.

The two women got their food and after a few minutes one of them called me over. She was pointing at the salad:

'Scuse me, mister, we only wanted two chicken sambos. What's with the bleedin flower sh*te?'

Overheard by Daniel O'Connor, pub in Dublin
Posted on Thursday, 12 May 2005

## 3-year-olds know everything

Was playing with my 3-year-old niece a few weeks ago. She had a board with the letters of the alphabet and little pictures of objects for each of the letters such as A for apple etc.

Me: 'What is 'M' for?'

Her: 'Mummy.'

Me: 'Well yes, but here 'M' is for mouse.'

Her: 'NO! 'M' is for mummy.'

Me: 'But lots of words start with 'M', like mouse, man, milk. What does milk start with then?'

Her (angrily walking away): 'Milk starts with cows!'

Overheard by Viv, my bro's house
Posted on Thursday, 12 May 2005

## Sweet smell of success

Was at Dublin Airport and my flight had been delayed so we had to wait several hours in the departure lounge. One young couple sitting near me had a little girl who, after waiting around for a few hours was becoming tired and emotional. She kept crying that she wanted sweets from the shop, while her mother refused to give in to the request and tried to calm her down.

Realising she wasn't going to win through complaining alone, the little girl began screaming, 'MUMMY DOES BIG SMELLY FARTS!' at the top of her voice.

She soon got her sweets.

Overheard by Jack Wade, Dublin Airport
Posted on Wednesday, 11 May 2005

## The Luas countryside service is delayed ...

While awaiting the Luas outside Heuston Station, a rather trollied looking fellow approached the Dublin Bus man who was just hanging around. The tram pulled in, and the drunk fella asked the bus man,

'Is this the Sligo train?'

Overheard by MC, outside Heuston Station
Posted on Wednesday, 11 May 2005

## The Hill's alive ...

Two Dublin football supporters passing comment on a rather portly member of the county team on Hill 16 a few years back:

Dub #1: 'Jayzis, yer man turns like the Titanic.'

Dub #2: 'Yeah, and he's got an arse like an iceberg as well!'

Overheard by Eamo, Hill 16
Posted on Wednesday, 11 May 2005

## No wonder she crashed

D4 girl #1: 'I crashed my car yesterday.'

D4 girl #2: 'Where?'

D4 girl #1: 'On the road!'

**Overheard by kicks, UCD**
Posted on Wednesday, 11 May 2005

## The nutty professor

Was in college studying computer maintenance. The professor was from Sallynoggin, a real Dublin aul fella. Anyways I asked him how to do a certain thing on the PC and he shouts down, 'RTFM' and I said, 'What do you mean RTFM?' and he replies in loud voice,

'READ THE F\*\*KING MANUAL!'

**Overheard by anon, FAS, Loughlinstown**
Posted on Tuesday, 10 May 2005

## The munchies

Chatting to one of my patients randomly one day, the conversation turns to drug addicts, and what a terrible affliction it is.

'I know,' says he, 'I was on the bus the other day and there was this strung-out fella, eatin' a Vienetta out of a bag like it was an ice-cream on a stick.'

I stifle a laugh, and try to maintain my professional facade. Contemplating the Vienetta for a minute, he then says,

'I mean, a f\*\*kin' Vienetta! That thing is for, like, six f\*\*kin' people!'

Overheard by Donal, dental surgery D2
Posted on Tuesday, 10 May 2005

## Office

At work recently a colleague rang the local Ink Cartridge Supplies called Mr Inky. When the person answered was female he got a little confused and said, 'Emmm, is that Mrs Inky?'

Overheard by Domanval, at work
Posted on Tuesday, 10 May 2005

## Boob talk

A few weeks back I found myself on the no. 38 bus going out to Blanchardstown. I happened to be sitting upstairs midway down the bus and for the best part of the journey all I could hear from the back seat was:

'Where's Mammy's diddies, where's Mammy's diddies, no, no you don't have diddies yet, you're too young, where's Mammy's diddies, where's Mammy's diddies, that's right, there's Mammy's diddies.'

Overheard by Shuggy, no. 38 bus
Posted on Tuesday, 10 May 2005

## Empty vessels

On the bus from Mullingar to Dublin driving down the quays at low tide:

Woman #1: 'The river is very low isn't it?'

Woman #2: 'Yeah I think they drain it every so often.'

Woman #1: 'Really? I wonder where they put it?'

The bloke sitting next to me looked at me in disbelief. I told him that, yes, I heard it too, which seemed to reassure him a bit.

Overheard by Val, Mullingar to Dublin bus

Posted on Tuesday, 10 May 2005

## WMDs

Walking down Dame Street one skanger yells across the street to another, 'Anto! Yer ma's a f\*\*king weapon!' . . . great stuff.

Overheard by Debo, Dame Street

Posted on Tuesday, 10 May 2005

## Mood swings

Walking along Sean McDermott Street on the way to work one sunny morning. Homeless guy looks up from reading his paper, smiles at me and practically shouts out, 'You're young, life is good, enjoy your youth!'

I replied, 'Thanks, I will.'

Very next morning the same guy, same place, looks up from his paper as I pass and says, 'F\*\*k off, you're only a b\*ll\*x, you're all the same ye f\*\*kin parasites.'

What can you say to that?

Overheard by Shwillo, corner of Sean McDermott and Buckingham Streets

Posted on Tuesday, 10 May 2005

# The potential dangers of the Irish Sea

On the DART home and a Dublin fella who could fairly be described as being hammered gets on. He starts talking to everyone and no one in particular and giving all manner of amusement to all.

In between offering advice to any celebrities on the train about giving autographs, and lamenting about local politicians not caring about recycling — 'Sure that's only a money-making scam anyway' — he stops to watch some windsurfers near Dun Laoghaire.

'Jaysus,' says he, 'it's a mad day for sorfin'. Imagine a big shark came along and ate them all.'

Pondering this for a while he concludes, 'That'd be f**kin' great!'

Overheard by Big T, on the DART on the way home
Posted on Monday, 9 May 2005


# Cheeky train fella

I was getting the DART from Greystones. I went to the counter and asked the uniformed guy for a 'ticket to Sandycove, please'. Hands me the ticket. I then asked politely, 'How long will the train be, do you know?'

He sits back on his chair and with a dead straight face said, 'About four or five carriages.'

I had to walk away!

Overheard by JH, Greystones
Posted on Monday, 9 May 2005

## Turd salad

While queuing in Avoca Handweavers at the weekend, I was shocked to learn that the enterprising folks in Avoca have in fact managed to manufacture and sell Turd Salad.

Lady in queue: 'I'll have shepherds pie, pasta salad and green salad.'

Assistant: 'Ma'am would you like a turd salad wit dat ... ?'

At which point at least 10 fellow onlookers buckled over with laughter.

Overheard by Tom, Avoca Handweavers
Posted on Monday, 9 May 2005

## Funny cos it's true

One night in a nightclub in Dublin, as the lights came on one guy screams,

'Oh my god, everyone's so ugly!'

The looks he got from the women!

Overheard by Anonymous, Spirit Nightclub
Posted on Sunday, 8 May 2005

## He does have a point

My girlfriend and I were waiting for the bus in town. She was leafing through a magazine that she bought. Then this old man came up to her, stared at her and said,

'You like looking through people's lives don't you?' and just stood in front of her staring at her.

Overheard by Andy, Nassau Street, waiting for no. 7 bus
Posted on Saturday, 7 May 2005

## Tastes like chicken

Bloke asks foreign chef in the canteen, 'What's that?' pointing to the food.

Foreign chef says: 'Churkey'.

Bloke says: 'Churkey? What's churkey?'

Foreign chef says: 'It's like chicken.'

Bloke then thought it was some weird turkey/chicken hybrid — when it was just turkey.

Overheard by mbv, canteen in work
Posted on Friday, 6 May 2005

# Dublin in the rare old days

Was walking home from school one day with a few friends and there was this old guy just sitting on the pavement reading the *Irish Times*. As we were going past he loudly remarked, 'Ah yes! Dublin in the rare old days, in the rare old days!'

Then presently went back to his paper.

Overheard by Clare, Griffith Avenue
Posted on Friday, 6 May 2005


# Up Cork, Up Meath and Up ...

All Ireland final day in 1999 and we were all dressed in red and white (obviously supporting Cork). Lovely day so we were outside the Hogan Stand Bar enjoying the craic and all that when a typical head-the-ball 'sales man' approached us.

Head-the-ball: 'Ye's from Cork' (obviously educated to associate red jerseys with Cork).

Us: 'We are.'

Next thing, a car load of Meath supporters drives past and one of them roars out, 'UP MEATH'.

Before any of us could think of anything to say back, Head-the-ball (roars), 'UP YOURS!'

Had everyone outside the pub rolling around laughing.

Overheard by Pat, Hogan Stand Bar
Posted on Friday, 6 May 2005

## The thin yellow line!

I was getting off the DART in Connolly when I heard the following announcement:

'Could all passengers on platform three please stand behind the yellow line,' to which no one moved, so the guy makes the announcement again, this time sounding a bit more irate. After no one moves, he decides to ditch the fake posh accent and yells,

'Could youse lot move behind the bleedin' line, I won't tell yis again!'

Overheard by K, Connolly Station
Posted on Thursday, 5 May 2005

## Some might say that son!

I'm living in Clonakilty nearly six years now and on a visit to Dublin a few years back decided to 'treat' my two kids to a bus run from Rialto into the city centre. Naturally, it being a novelty, it was up the stairs and to the front seats.

As we crossed O'Connell Bridge my little lad Sean, who was just a babe in arms when we left Dublin, saw the Daniel O'Connell monument.

'Look Dad,' he said, 'Superman!'

Overheard by Hugh, no. 19A bus from Rialto
Posted on Thursday, 5 May 2005

## Don't whistle while you work

Working on a building site on the quays, dossing around one day with the other builders. There was a crane banksman standing there with his walkie-talkie, a real Dub this guy was, and seeing as it was nearing the weekend I was in a good mood. So I started to sing to no one in particular,

'He's a crane op-er-ator, craaaaaane oper-atorrrr,'

(to the tune of smooth operator) and the banksman shouted,

'Are yew foookin BENT or wha?'

Overheard by Jiggers, the quays<br>Posted on Thursday, 5 May 2005

## Sri Lanka

Students: 'We're collecting money for Sri Lanka, for charity.'

Student 1: 'Who is Sri Lanka?'

Student 2: 'I'm not sure, I think she's famous.'

Student 1: 'Yeah I've heard the name somewhere before. Is she a singer?'

Overheard by Michelle, St Mary's Holy Faith, Killester<br>Posted on Tuesday, 3 May 2005

## Help the aged

My uncle is a landlord, and he has some elderly tenants. When the euro came in, an elderly lady was complaining about it to him because she couldn't get her head around the conversion:

'Why can't they wait 'til the old people die before they bring it in?' she asked.

Overheard by Anthony, Terenure<br>Posted on Tuesday, 3 May 2005

# Eaten alive

While walking behind a funeral cortège in a Dublin graveyard, a rat scurried across the grass. One old lady said to another,

'I wouldn't like to be buried in this place, you'd be eaten alive.'

Overheard by Mick, Mount Jerome
Posted on Tuesday, 3 May 2005

# It's a miracle!

My brother arrives into Dublin Airport and is dying for a pee. He makes it to the Gents but there's a huge queue. He sees that the disabled toilet is free so he decides to leg it in before he wets himself. After relieving himself he's coming out the door when an auld lad still waiting in the queue for the Gents sarcastically declares,

'JAYSUS, it's a f\*\*king miracle!'

Good 'old style' Irish humour! My brother knew he was home!

Overheard by Grainne, Dublin Airport
Posted on Monday, 2 May 2005

# 'Just ignore him'

Two girls in a cinema in Dublin in the 60s:

'Oh Jaysus, the guy beside me is playin wit himself.'

Friend: 'Just ignore him.'

'I can't, he's usin my hand!'

Overheard by Joe, my aunt heard this in the
Metropole in Dublin in the 60s
Posted on Monday, 2 May 2005

## Parental problems

Two aul dears queuing for the no. 27 bus. Just caught the end of the conversation:

Old dear #1: 'Sure whoaya tellin. De kids dees days is terrible bold.'

Old dear #2: 'And ye know it's not de parents I blame, it's de mudders an fadders.'

Overheard by Anna, town
Posted on Sunday, 1 May 2005

## Sausage discrimination

Myself and my flat mate decided to pay a visit to the new shopping centre in Dundrum on the opening day. In Tesco we decide to get one of those sample tasters (Tesco sausages) from the stall that they have for promotion of the food. Obviously being students we approached the woman at the stall:

Woman: 'Are yeee stoodens, lads?'

Me: 'Students? Yes we are.'

Woman: 'Sorry we can't serve stoodens, talk to head awffice if you have a problem.'

They refused to serve us a piece of Tesco finest sausages!

Overheard by a.m, Tesco, Dundrum
Posted on Friday, 29 April 2005

$x = crazy, y = old guy, z = 13a,$
$x+y+z=?$

So I'm sat on the no. 13A bus on my way into town when this old guy in his 80s sits down next to me.

Old guy: 'Alright?'

Me (nod politely not really wanting to get into a conversation).

Old guy: 'Do you know any algebra?'

Me (feeling confused and positive I've misheard him): 'Sorry?'

Old guy: 'ALGEBRA! You know x's y's that kind of thing?'

Me: 'Well I did a bit in school but that's a good while ago.'

Old guy: 'Jesus it's fierce handy stuff. Fierce handy stuff.'

And with that he turns away and doesn't say another word.

Overheard by Mic, no. 13A bus
Posted on Friday, 29 April 2005

## Stupid computers

Student: 'Computers can be so stupid sometimes!'

Computer programming lecturer: 'Computers are only as stupid as the people who put the information in!'

Student (correcting himself): 'Yeah ... suppose! Computer programmers are so stupid.'

Overheard by Locks, computer lab, DIT, Aungier Street

Posted on Friday, 29 April 2005

## Did you make it yourself?

While bringing my dog (a Kerry Blue terrier) for a walk in the local park, I encountered the following from a passer-by:

Passer-by: 'That's a gorgeous dog! Is it a he or a she?'

Me: 'Thanks, it's a he.'

Passer-by: 'It's very unique, what make is it?'

Me: 'Eh ... a Kerry Blue terrier.'

Overheard by Pete, Bushy Park, Rathfarnham

Posted on Friday, 29 April 2005

## Putting the vegetarian argument to rest

Mother with her young son and teenage daughter on the bus into town for a day out. An argument ensues:

Young Boy: 'Mam, can we go to McDonald's later?'

Mam: 'We'll see, don't forget that Cliona's a vegetarian so she may not want to eat there.'

Teenage Girl: 'There's no way we're going to McDonald's.'

Young Boy: 'That's not fair, anyway what's wrong with eating meat?'

Teenage Girl: 'It's cruelty to animals.'

Young Boy: 'If we aren't supposed to eat animals, then why are they made out of meat?'

Teenage Girl — eyes to heaven.

Overheard by Rob, no. 15B bus
Posted on Friday, 29 April 2005

## Stones

A few months ago I overheard two auld fellas in a city pub talking about an African woman who was to be deported. She did not wish to leave Ireland, claiming that she would be stoned to death in her own country after being found guilty of committing adultery. One auld fella says,

'I hope they don't bring that in here or they'll run out of stones.'

Overheard by DW, Foggy Dew pub
Posted on Friday, 29 April 2005

## Garda exaggeration

Sitting in Tallaght District Court as you do, awaiting my own wrist slapping, a young fellah was up before the court on possession of cannabis resin.

Garda: 'The defendant was found in possession of approximately 20 grams of cannabis resin.'

Judge: 'In layman's terms about how much is that?'

Garda: 'It's enough for about 70 cannabis cigarettes, your honour.'

Defendant (in absolute shock): 'What the f\*\*k are you smoking, you must be doing serious top loadin?'

Court and congregated skangers: — Hysterics

Judge: — Not impressed

Overheard by cormdogg, Tallaght District Court
Posted on Thursday, 28 April 2005

## Higher de musik down

On the no. 27 bus a bunch of young skangers are sitting down the back annoying everyone with the hard house blaring out of their tinny stereo. One of their phones starts ringing and the owner takes a look at the caller ID screen and says:

'Jaysus, it's me ma, higher de musik down, willya!'

Overheard by Fenster, no. 27 bus from Coolock
Posted on Thursday, 28 April 2005

## Free lift

Having snuck into the Trinity Ball and decided it wasn't worth it after all, me and a friend were heading for the exit behind a couple of posh gals, with their sandals in their hands.

We pass by a girl with vomit stains down her swanky dress and still with a beer in one hand, being loaded into a wheelchair by the bored looking ambulance fellas. One of the girls in front of us says,

'Jesus look at her. Lucky cow, she'll get a lift home in the ambulance.'

Overheard by Ruffy, by the Rubrics in Trinners
Posted on Thursday, 28 April 2005

## Never a truer word was spoken

One strung-out skanger passing another strung-out skanger at a bus stop in Irishtown.

Skanger 1: 'Where ya goin?'

Skanger 2: 'Nowhere.'

Overheard by Katie, Irishtown
Posted on Thursday, 28 April 2005

## Colour dilemma

'I don't want cream. Cream is for girls. Girls are gay. I'm not gay. I want black. Black is deadly.'

Overheard by Giggler, 7-year-old telling his ma his choice of Holy Communion suit colours on the no. 51B bus, Clondalkin
Posted on Thursday, 28 April 2005

# A glass of Dun Laoghaire

Two middle-aged English couples came into a
bar and asked the barman did he know any
good ports, to which the barman replied, 'Yes,
Dun Laoghaire.'

Tourist: 'Ok, we'll have two of those and two
Guinness, please.'

Overheard by katy, The Auld Dubliner, Temple Bar
Posted on Thursday, 28 April 2005

# Breadless sandwich

Me: 'Can I have a brown bread sandwich?'

Girl serving: 'We have no brown bread.'

Me: 'Can I have a roll then?'

Girl serving: 'We have no rolls.'

Me: 'Can I have a white bread sandwich or a bap
or something?'

Girl serving: 'We have no white bread or baps.'

Me: 'What have you?'

Girl serving: 'Wraps.'

Overheard by Stephen, sandwich bar in Fare Play shop in Esso
garage at Loughlinstown
Posted on Wednesday, 27 April 2005

# Tarantula rain

Was sitting in my sister's car coming to work one
morning, when she starts complaining about the
dirt of the car. I asked her how it got so dirty.
Her reply:

'I drove to Ashbourne last night in the tarantula rain.'

As opposed to torrential!

Overheard by Anonymous, on way to work!
Posted on Wednesday, 27 April 2005

## Some people have it tough

Two Dublin 4 women in conversation on bus:

D4 #1: 'Have you been away at all?'

D4 #2: 'No just a few short breaks, nothing major.'

D4 #1: 'Where did you go?'

D4 #2: 'We were in New York for a weekend at Christmas then for Valentine's we went to Paris and at Easter we had a week in West Cork.'

D4 #1: 'I bet you can't wait to get away again?'

D4 #2: 'Oh yeah, like a real holiday abroad.'

Overheard by anonymous, no. 46A bus
Posted on Wednesday, 27 April 2005

## The weathermen

In college I overheard two lads from Galway talking about a holiday one of them had just come back from:

Lad #1: 'So, how did you find the heat?'

Lad #2: 'Ah, shur it wasn't the heat, it was the humanity that would kill ya!'

TV3 Weather might have some competition on their hands!

Overheard by Anonymous, DIT, Aungier Street
Posted on Tuesday, 26 April 2005

## Geographically in limbo

Sitting in one of the larger lecture theatres in Bolton Street at the information sessions they do for Leaving Cert students. After a gruelling two hour talk about the relative merits of studying engineering in the DIT, the chairman asks anyone with any questions to submit them to the panel by writing them down on a piece of paper and passing them down to the front.

My mate starts writing frantically, and passes his question forward. The chairman collects it and reads it out:

'Is there any relationship between geography and engineering?'

To which the same chairman replied, with the sternest of looks in the direction of my mate,

'Well you found your way here to the lecture didn't you?'

Overheard by RonnieDrewsDublin, DIT, Bolton Street
Posted on Tuesday, 26 April 2005

## Where's a revolving door when you need one?

While walking out of a hotel lobby with a friend and her mother, her mother was having a hard time trying to pull open the door. So my friend says to her mother,

'Mam, it says PUSH on the door!'

To which her mother replies,

'I know it says PUSH but it doesn't say which way!'

Overheard by Barry, Bewley's Hotel
Posted on Tuesday, 26 April 2005

## Never assume a Dublin bus driver knows the way!

I was getting a replacement bus from Portmarnock DART Station to the city centre as there are no DART services at the weekends on the northside. It was a Sunday afternoon and I was the only passenger on the bus. There was the inspector/supervisor guy talking to the bus driver who was obviously foreign. I listened more carefully and realised the inspector guy was giving the bus driver directions! I immediately thought … feck!

Then, to my great amusement, the inspector turned to me and asked me, 'Young man, do you know where you're goin?' To which I replied, 'Yeah.'

He then said, 'You wuddin mind keepin an eye on this lad and showing him the way, wud ya?' !?

Turned out the bus driver was from Guatemala and I had a great chat with him and we ended up going a little bit out of the way, but it was one of my more enjoyable Dublin Bus experiences!

Overheard by Anonymous, Portmarnock
Posted on Tuesday, 26 April 2005

## Rugby goys

Was on a packed Luas on the way into work the other day, and we pull up to Ranelagh. This jock in a suit and tie is trying to get on, but there was no room, so next thing he says, 'Roysh goys rugby squeeze' and he forces himself onto the

Luas. He spent the rest of the journey into Stephen's Green muttering to himself.

Extraordinary!

Overheard by Chris, on the Luas (Ranelagh)
Posted on Tuesday, 26 April 2005

## The wristband inspector

A curious 'head-the-ball' impatiently waiting for a bus decides to question a young student (who knows it's probably in his best interests to answer) about his array of wristbands.

Head-the-ball: 'What are they about bud?'

Student: 'Em just different charities.'

Head-the-ball: 'Yeah? What's the yellow one for?'

Student: 'It's for a cancer charity.'

Head-the-ball: 'What's the white one for?'

Student: 'It's an anti-racism bracelet.'

Head-the-ball: 'What's the black one for?'

Student: 'It comes with the white one.'

Head-the-ball: 'What's the blue one for?'

Student: 'The blue one's for anti-bullying and the red one's for Childline.'

Head-the-ball: 'Do you have any more?'

Student: 'No, that's it.'

Head-the-ball: 'Good man.'

Overheard by Jimmy, bus stop outside IT, Tallaght
Posted on Monday, 25 April 2005

# Have a seat

Imagine a nice night out with friends in town in a bar I won't mention. You go to the loo and notice a girl sitting on the sink and think, oh there's loads of seats outside, then you realise she is sitting there for a reason. All the loos are full and she happily tells you, 'Jesus I was dying.'

Disturbed? I think so!

Overheard by saoirse, pub in Dublin
Posted on Monday, 25 April 2005

# Only trying to help

Sitting on NiteLink at 2 a.m. trying to keep myself to myself. When approached by a young Dublin lad on his way home, suitably refreshed after a night on the Beer.

Dub: 'Does dis bus stop in Palmerstown?'

Me: 'I dunno, why don't you ask the driver?'

Dub: 'Ahh why don't you ask me bollix!'

Me: ?

Overheard by Niall, NiteLink to Lucan
Posted on Monday, 25 April 2005

# Dog story

'Rover! Cameer ya bollix!'

Overheard by Barbara Woodhouse, street
Posted on Friday, 22 April 2005

## Decent bloke

Girl: 'Giz a kiss.'

Bloke: 'Let me swally me phlegm first.'

*Overheard by Trixibell, Talbot Street*
*Posted on Friday, 22 April 2005*

## Ireland of the welcomes!

In Roddy Boland's in Rathmines one night I overheard a group of Italian guys (tourists) trying to chat up two Irish girls and not getting very far. One of the Italians started waxing lyrical about one of the girls and her 'beautiful pale skin' and said,

'In my country, you would be a princess.'

To which the Irish girl replied,

'And in my country, you'd work in a chipper, now f**k off.'

*Overheard by Kaz, Roddy Boland's*
*Posted on Friday, 22 April 2005*

## Handbags

At a well-known tourist bar in Temple Bar the musicians are trying to get the crowd going:

MC: 'Is there anyone here from Germany?'

Germans: 'Yeahhhhh!'

MC: 'Is there anyone here from England?'

English: 'Yeahhhhh!'

Irish: 'Boooo!'

MC: 'Is there anyone here from Cork?'

Cork People: 'Yeahhhhh!' etc. etc.

MC: 'Is there anyone here from Limerick?'

Limerick People: 'Yeahhhh!'

MC: 'Well the rest of yiz, mind your bleedin' handbags!'

Overheard by Mick, Oliver St John Gogarty's

Posted on Friday, 22 April 2005

## Irish law is never black and white

In one of the Dublin district courts during a hearing the injured party is being questioned by the defence barrister. The barrister is really trying to put pressure on the man and questions whether he can identify his client who allegedly assaulted him. The injured party is sitting in the witness box and without flinching points across the room and says loudly,

'Yer man there, the black fella.'

The defence barrister loses the rag and begins ranting about being prejudicial to his client's skin colour and so forth. The barrister continues along this line of attack and says indignantly to the injured party who is still in the witness box,

'Can you identify the man in this courtroom who you allege assaulted you, without referring to his skin colour?'

The injured party looks up at the judge and then at the barrister, shrugs and says, 'Yeah.'

The barrister asks him to do so. The injured party points again across the courtroom and says,

'Yer man sitting over there between the two white blokes.'

Overheard by Anonymous, Dublin District Court

Posted on Thursday, 21 April 2005

# I don't give a Ratzinger

I was in a queue in Tesco in town the other day after work when I heard two lads talking about the new Pope:

'What do you think about the new Pope?' said one to the other.

The reply: 'I don't give a Ratzinger ...'

Boom boom!

Overheard by John, Tesco
Posted on Thursday, 21 April 2005

# Good news for Robbie Keane then

Overheard two lads talking about football:

Lad #1: 'I think Robbie Keane has lost his impotence' (meant to say *impetus*).

Lad #2: 'Impotence!? Will you stop using big words for feck sake' (failing to pick up on his mate's error).

Overheard by Sean, Hanlon's pub
Posted on Thursday, 21 April 2005

## Grand opening

Was at my grandmother's funeral when during a quiet part of the mass my daughter (three years old) asked,

'Daddy, when are they opening the box?'

Overheard by Roy, church in Raheny
Posted on Wednesday, 20 April 2005

## Country girl in the big smoke

Country girl gets on no. 16 bus and asks driver how much is the fare.

Driver replies, 'Where are you going?'

Country girl says, 'To get my hair done!'

Overheard by Helen, no. 16 bus
Posted on Wednesday, 20 April 2005

## Red sky at night ...

In the back of a cab on a summer's night going up the quays, it was a beautiful evening with a red sky.

'Red sky at night ...' said my friend Neil, waiting for one of us to finish the well-known phrase.

'... Tallaght's on fire,' intercepted the cab driver.

Hearty laughs all round.

Overheard by Ems, back of a cab
Posted on Wednesday, 20 April 2005

# A real breakfast roll

While in a Spar shop a young shop assistant was serving me at the deli counter. I asked her for a breakfast roll; she was obviously new to the job and went to her boss. I missed some of the conversation but I did hear her ask the boss,

'So will I give yer wan cornflakes or rice krispies in a bread roll or somtin, I haven't a clue wah she's on abou?'

She had failed to notice the hot counter …

Overheard by squeegie, Spar shop
Posted on Wednesday, 20 April 2005

# Alternative history

Was walking past the GPO and an English bloke was showing off his knowledge of Irish history to a couple of English girls.

'That building is the GPO, it was where the Irish had their revolution in 1910!'

Well, he wasn't that far off!

Overheard by penny, GPO
Posted on Wednesday, 20 April 2005

# Chugger excuse

For those of you who don't know, a 'Chugger' is an in-your-face 'Charity Mugger'. One of those over-confident, dreadlocked, hoody-wearing, studenty-type, 'out-of-work actor type' people who stands in the street with a clipboard soliciting donations to the Feline Liberation Army or some other worthy cause.

Scene: A chugger approaches two lads strolling through Temple Bar:

Chugger: 'Hi goys! Do you have a moment?'

Guy #1: 'Eh ...'

Chugger: 'Roysh, what we do is ...'

Guy #2: 'I already have an account with this charity.'

Chugger: 'Oh, well done.' (Then turning his attention to guy #2) 'How about yourself?'

Guy #2 (sheepishly): 'So do I.'

Overheard by Pete, Temple Bar (where else?)
Posted on Wednesday, 20 April 2005

# The real Gaelic football?

On the Aircoach heading over the Royal Canal with a vista of Croke Park in the distance, one Spanish guy — appearing all-knowledgeable about Dublin — turns to his newcomer friend and, pointing, says,

'That's where Celtic play ...'

Overheard by Nicola, Aircoach
Posted on Wednesday, 20 April 2005

# De BIG leeher o' milk

Girl at petrol station to shop assistant who has brought her order of a 'leeher o' milk' to the hatch:

'Are ya f\*\*kin' deaf or wha? I wanted de BIG leeher.'

And off she went a moment later as happy as Larry with her 2-litre carton!

Overheard by Mary, Clondalkin petrol station
Posted on Tuesday, 19 April 2005

## Seen through a child's eyes!

A young boy was in mass with his granny the other day and he insisted on sitting in the middle of the aisle directly in front of the altar. When his granny tried to drag him in to sit beside her, the little boy turned around and told her that he was sitting in the middle,

'So God could get a better view of him!'

Overheard by Emma, mass in Blackrock
Posted on Tuesday, 19 April 2005

## Trivial Pursuit

Our friends were staying with us for a weekend. We were pretty broke so we decided we'd stay in and have a few drinks AND buy Trivial Pursuit ... how exciting! We visited Argos for our purchase. While paying for it at the till, the cashier verified my purchase ... 'Trivall Pursue'.

Overheard by Brenda, Argos, Blanchardstown
Posted on Tuesday, 19 April 2005

## Fingers for toes

Working in Simon Harts shoe shop on Henry Street I had a foreign lady come up to me and say,

'I think I need another size, my fingers are too tight in this one.'

Overheard by Gillian, Simon Harts, Henry Street
Posted on Tuesday, 19 April 2005

## Geography and History lessons needed

As I was crossing College Green last Saturday, I overheard a young Dubliner say to her friend, 'Do you know where you are now?' to which the friend, presumably from outside Dublin, replied 'Nope.' So the Dub said, sweeping her arm in the direction of the Bank of Ireland and Trinity,

'The Four Courts!'

Overheard by Aoife, College Green
Posted on Tuesday, 19 April 2005

## Sixteen Chapel, Rome

Asked my 6-year-old son what he learned at school today. He replied,

'They were picking the new Pope in the "sixteen chapel"!'

Overheard by Larry, at the school gate
Posted on Tuesday, 19 April 2005

## Irish queen

Walking down Pearse Street the other day and to my utter annoyance I heard one American tourist say to the other,

'Does the Queen rule here?'

Overheard by taytos, Pearse Street
Posted on Tuesday, 19 April 2005

# Good Friday Agreement

A friend of mine was explaining to an African work colleague in Ballyfermot the Christian calendar, and all the holidays and feast days. He was going over Shrove Tuesday, Ash Wednesday, Palm Sunday etc. When he reached Good Friday, the African colleague butted in,

'Yes, I know this holiday — this is the anniversary of peace in Northern Ireland, so we all get a holiday.'

[Good Friday Agreement!]

Overheard by Jason T. Flamingo, work in Ballyfermot
Posted on Tuesday, 19 April 2005

# Point of no return

A true blue Dublin elderly couple walked up to the ticket window at the DART station. They looked a little confused — like maybe they don't use the DART that much — and whispered among themselves for a few seconds.

Eventually the man says to the ticket guy, 'I need two return tickets.'

Ticket guy: 'Where to?'

Old guy: 'Here!'

Overheard by Dermot, Kilbarrack DART Station
Posted on Tuesday, 19 April 2005

# Ah Jaws'us!

Walking over the Ha'penny Bridge, a mum and her kid were in front of me ... the kid is crying.

Mum: 'If you don' bleedin' shuddup I'll throw you to the sharks!'

Overheard by Jemima, Ha'penny Bridge
Posted on Monday, 18 April 2005

## Loik!

D4 head (wearing a bright yellow shirt):

'Loik what is up with pink shirts lately! Loik do fellas not want to show their masculinity or something?'

Overheard by Denver, Grafton Street
Posted on Monday, 18 April 2005

## Those PlayStations

A commonly heard comment from GAA people in conversations on the debate of Croke Park on the radio over the last few days:

GAA man: 'The GAA has done a lot for the children of this country. Our activities keep them away from drink, drugs and playstations ...'

Overheard by Leo, Dublin Radio
Posted on Monday, 18 April 2005

## One of the lad(ie)s

Dublin Airport, off on holidays to Portugal with the lads, when my mate was next in line for passport control.

'Ever been abroad before?' the passport controller asked.

'No, I've always been a man!' came the reply.

Kicked off the holiday! Absolute classic!

Overheard by BianoBoy, Dublin Airport
Posted on Monday, 18 April 2005


# The leaning tower of Eiffel

Sitting in Arnott's café and there is this fella there obviously taking his elderly mother out for some Sunday shopping. Over a cup of coffee he's showing her photos from a recent trip:

'Now ma, there's the Eiffel Tower,' he says as he passes over a photo.

After a quick look at the photo she replies, 'Oh they've stopped it leaning so, that's good.'

Overheard by Stephen, Arnott's café
Posted on Monday, 18 April 2005

# Not so hard to get into college after all ...

Overheard two girls on the bus discussing college recently.

Girl #1: 'So are there more guys or girls on your course then?'

Girl #2: 'Definitely more girls ... I'd say it'd be 65:55 ...'

The correction never came.

Overheard by Fembot, no. 16A bus

Posted on Monday, 18 April 2005

# 'A test bus'

On the no. 45 bus, a route which takes in some of Dublin's leafier suburbs. Up the front of the top deck of the bus was an American family, taking it all in. Anyone who knows this route will be familiar with the sound of the branches from the overhanging trees brushing and thumping the side of the bus.

This sparked a vocal debate among the Americans about how the trees were cut. In the end they settled on the theory that a 'test bus' which had a kind of rotating saw on the top corner, must go out every morning to cut the branches back ...

Overheard by The Jackal, no. 45 bus

Posted on Monday, 18 April 2005

# Wrong sport

Overheard on the way to a canoe water polo championship.

Woman to her friend: 'But I don't understand how they get the horses into the water …'

Overheard by Ol, in Dublin
Posted on Monday, 18 April 2005

# Radio GAA GAA

I was at a GAA club football match and quite near me was a young man listening to the radio. He was listening to pop music on 2FM. That day there also happened to be quite a big inter-county match taking place in Croke Park. A middle-aged man sitting in front of me, obviously curious as to how the big game was panning out, turned to the young man and asked,

'Can you get Telefis Eireann on that yoke?'

Overheard by Finian Murray, local GAA club
Posted on Monday, 18 April 2005

# Vindaloo and Guinness

On a packed train and there was somebody who obviously had been eating Vindaloo and had gallons of Guinness the night before — the stench was unreal! This old lady got so annoyed and screamed all over the carriage,

'Can the person who is farting please stop; you're turning my god damn stomach.'

At this the carriage of people fell around
laughing …

Overheard by Dearbhla, on the DART heading into work
Posted on Monday, 18 April 2005


# Corrugation of Kids

A neighbour of ours who lives in a corner house
was complaining about kids hanging around at
the side of her house. She asked my Ma why the
kids had to 'corrugate' outside her house all the
time.

Overheard by Jimmy, Finglas
Posted on Sunday, 17 April 2005


# Didn't lick it off the stones

A friend of mine, teaching junior infants in
Tallaght, asked a mother to come and see her
because she was concerned about the bad
language being used by one particular child.
Every day at breaktime when she asked the
children to sit down so they could have some
milk and biscuits, the little girl would say,

'F**k you and your milk and biscuits, I'm
playing.'

She told the mother what was happening and
the mother paused for a moment.

'Diya know wha ti do,' said the mother, 'f**k
her, don't give 'er any, the ungrateful little get.'

Overheard by Anonymous, school in Tallaght
Posted on Sunday, 17 April 2005

# Thrilled and dilated

Working as an EMT on a Dublin ambulance, I was bringing a 16-year-old girl to the Rotunda Hospital.

'Would you say you're dilated?' I asked her. To which she replied,

'Dy-lay-rah? I'm over the f**kin moon!'

Overheard, Dublin ambulance by Sheller
Posted on Sunday, 17 April 2005

# Worldly mothers part III

Watching the Ireland v England Six Nations match with my family, the camera zooms in on Roy Keane in the crowd.

Dad goes, 'Wudja look who it is!'

Mum (sincerely) goes, 'What's Charlie Bird doing at a rugby match?'

Overheard by dani o'meara, sa bhaile
Posted on Sunday, 17 April 2005

# Dairy-pod

I was walking through my bro's school with a stick of butter and this kid walked over to me and said, 'Oh deadly, how much songs does that hold?'

Overheard by Poj, Scoil Mobhi
Posted on Sunday, 17 April 2005

# A reasonable threat

Mammy: 'If you're not good for your mammy, I'll put you in a black sack and leave you in the mountains.'

Overheard by Jenny, no. 3 Ballymun bus
Posted on Sunday, 17 April 2005

# A '10 minute' '15 minute' break

Musician: 'I'm just taking a quick 10 minute break, I'll be back in about 15 minutes.'

Overheard by Brian, Three Rock pub
Posted on Sunday, 17 April 2005

# Who-dini?

I was buying a scratch card (classy!) in downtown newsagent. 'What type of card dja want love?' 'A winning one,' I reply wittily. 'Ahh come on now love — I'm not bleedin' Houdini!'

Overheard by Sunniva, Dame Street
Posted on Sunday, 17 April 2005

# Just plain disgusting

A gang of oul fellas leaving the Black Sheep absolutely plastered. One stops and starts vomiting behind a car. 'Will ya hurry up for f**k sake, Deco, wor bleedin freezin.' Deco shouts back, 'Jaysus will yis wait til I get me teeth.'

With that he fishes his false teeth out of the pool of vomit and puts them straight back into his mouth and says, 'Are we gettin a burger or wha?'

Overheard by Anonymous, Black Sheep
Posted on Saturday, 16 April 2005

## 2 weeks in Pavarotti — priceless

I work with two oul lads and one comes in the other day delighted with himself, announces he's after getting two tickets for Pavarotti. To which the other replied,

'Jaysus, dat's great, are yis goin' for one week or two?'

Overheard by Dave, Tayto
Posted on Saturday, 16 April 2005

## Meath Hospital

Worried about a series of nose bleeds, my friend went to see his local doctor in Inchicore. When the doctor suggested that he would probably need to go to Meath Hospital (in Dublin of course), he replied,

'Is there any chance I could go to one in Dublin?'

Overheard by Dave, Inchicore
Posted on Saturday, 16 April 2005

## Brains from the 'Brack

My football team recently got a new manager from Ballybrack. At one of his first training sessions he was taking the warm-up, wanting us to increase the pace. He instructed, 'Right lads, up to three quarter pace … 87 per cent.'

We have lost our first five games this season …

Overheard by Blackadder, training in Ballybrack
Posted on Saturday, 16 April 2005

## Cruel but funny

A couple of years ago I was waiting for a bus to Maynooth at the Abbey Street terminus. A very short guy walked by wearing a Dublin Bus uniform, when some bloke shouts out,

'Ere Mister, are you a mini-bus driver?'

Overheard by Mick, waiting in line for the bus to Maynooth
Posted on Saturday, 16 April 2005

## Angina luv?

I'm a medical secretary and last week the doctor I work for was stunned when, while giving an examination to a woman who had complained of chest pains, he murmured to himself, 'Angina,' to which she replied,

'Enjoyin' it? I'm bleedin' lovin' it!'

Overheard by Anna, Mater Hospital
Posted on Saturday, 16 April 2005

# Fussy

Two 'yaw roights', dolled up to the nines, admiring each other, drinking mudshakes and waiting to be asked to dance. Eventually an average looking guy approached one of them.

Guy: 'Grea' in here isn it, de ye wan ti dance?'

The girl looked at him scathingly from head to toe and replied as bitchily as she could, 'No thanks, I'm fussy about who I dance with,' and then smirked at her friend.

Quick as a flash the guy replied, 'I'm not love, that's why I asked you.'

Overheard by x, Turks Head
Posted on Saturday, 16 April 2005

# Nice

Two culchie women choosing soft drinks — one has a Fanta, the other a Sprite Zero.

Sprite Zero Lady: 'Sure get this one, it's meant ta be good for ya.'

Fanta Lady: 'Ah but I like this one better.'

Sprite Zero Lady: 'But this one's got zero carolies!'

(misspelling intentional)

Overheard by S, Tesco in the Dundrum Town Centre
Posted on Saturday, 16 April 2005

# Language barriers

I was working in Arnotts (Sports Shoes) last summer, when a young Chinese couple came up to me to enquire about a size of a pair of runners. The man seemed to be impatient and in a hurry. I asked him, 'Are you rushing?' to which the two of them looked at me in disgust and replied out loud,

'No, we are Chinese!'

Overheard by Sean, Arnotts
Posted on Friday, 15 April 2005

## Em, water I guess

Group of Kerry lads walking in the Clonskeagh entrance of UCD, first day of college; one of the lads turns, looks up at the large tall structure and asks,

'Lads, what's stored in the water tower?'

1st Class Honours!

Overheard by J Perryman, UCD
Posted on Friday, 15 April 2005

## Lookin great!

Went to the toilet in the Windjammer pub, Townsend Street. From the cubicle I overheard two women:

Younger woman: 'Jaysis, Margaret, you're lookin great! What age are you now?'

Older woman (proudly): 'I'm 74.'

Younger woman: 'Jaysis, that's the age Rob's mother was when she died!'

Overheard by Anonymous, Windjammer pub
Posted on Friday, 15 April 2005

# Seven Letters — 12 Across

While listening to a couple of mates today doing a crossword at lunchtime:

Crossword guy: 'Capital city of Cyprus?'

Friend: 'How many letters?'

Crossword guy: 'Seven.'

Friend: 'Any letters?'

Crossword guy: 'Yep, third letter is "C".'

Friend: 'Any other info?'

Crossword guy: 'Yep, it's 12 Across.'

Friend: 'Oh, Nicosia!'

Overheard by Paddy, Hewlett Packard canteen
Posted on Friday, 15 April 2005

# Croke Park (a heated debate)

Man #1: 'So do you hope the GAA vote yes to change Rule 42?'

Man #2: 'What? What the f**k you on about?'

Overheard by Macker, Boardwalk
Posted on Friday, 15 April 2005

# No, we don't sell dictionaries

Customer: 'Is that sign going to be permanent?'

Cashier: 'For a little while.'

Overheard by Dec, Eason's
Posted on Friday, 15 April 2005

# Jesus saves

Priest tells joke at mass: 'The devil and Jesus were both doing work on their computer, then there's a power cut. The devil loses all his work but Jesus doesn't, because Jesus never forgets to save!'

Overheard by Greg, mass in Coolock
Posted on Friday, 15 April 2005

# Boy or girl?

Heard a girl answer her phone in the waiting room of Holles Street Maternity Hospital:

'Well, tell me, am I an Auntie or an Uncle?'

Overheard by Roy, Holles Street
Posted on Thursday, 14 April 2005

# Engineering solutions

I was sitting on a plane in Dublin Airport recently, about to take off for Prague, when one of the air hostesses noticed a panel above my seat was hanging down. She said we couldn't take off until this was sorted by an engineer. Ten minutes later, the engineer comes on. He has a look at the panel while stroking his chin. He then walks off and comes back 15 minutes later with Sellotape and begins to tape the panel back in place.

Someone says sarcastically, 'Do you want a piece of chewing gum just to make doubly sure?'

The engineer laughs and says, 'You think this is bad! You should see the wing!'

Overheard by Yossarian, sitting on Aer Lingus flight on runway at Dublin Airport

Posted on Thursday, 14 April 2005

## No minerils!

I was in the Liffey Valley Shopping Centre during Christmas and decided to visit the 'Food Court'. The place was chock a block with queues of people. Unfortunately McDonald's had run out of soft drinks and instead of the expected 'McDonald's would like to apologise for the lack of soft drinks and encourage you to try our delicious shakes etc.' message, an employee was standing in front of the queue to deliver a special announcement:

'Dere's no point en' queuin', we've no minerils!'

Overheard by Anthony, Liffey Valley

Posted on Thursday, 14 April 2005

## Smoking's bad for your feet

I was smoking on the upper deck of the no. 17A. The bus driver comes over the speaker and says, 'We would like to remind passengers that smoking is not allowed on the bus.'

I was just putting it out when he continued, 'Smoking causes blisters on your feet when you have to get out and walk.'

Overheard by Annmarie, no. 17A bus

Posted on Thursday, 14 April 2005

## Taxi driver wisdom

Getting a taxi home from town after being at a gig in memory of Phil Lynott of Thin Lizzy. The driver was (of course) a Lizzy expert. His opinion of Phil Lynott was:

'Ah yeahhhh, Philo was the only really COOL Irish rock star, yenowadimean? Like, Bono ... he's just a f**kin social worker with a singin' career.'

Overheard by flish, taxi
Posted on Thursday, 14 April 2005

## Tax the passengers

On the no. 41A bus heading for town, two guys got on in their 'nice' shell tracksuits and caps at 45 degree angles. One of the guys spies a poster on the bus for 'bustext' to which he loudly proclaims,

'BUS-TAXT? Look at that, the gov-dern-ment trying to rip us off again!'

Overheard by Anonymous, no. 41A bus
Posted on Thursday, 14 April 2005

## Allegators

Working in Sheriff Street for An Post. We had a serious union meeting where the head of the branch was giving out that someone was making allegations about him ... he said,

'If I catch the allegators there's gonna be trouble!'

Enough said ...

Overheard by Fergus, Sheriff Street (An Post)
Posted on Wednesday, 13 April 2005

# Visce?

A typical Trinity/D4 toff asking a lunch lady in the Buttery:

Toff: 'Sorry, is there anywhere I can get wawter?'

Lady: 'Sardy, love?'

Toff: 'I want wawter.'

Lady: 'WHA?'

Toff: 'WAWTER.'

This went on for an amazingly long time till she finally copped it and said, 'Ohhh … whaaaaaaaateh,' with a big smile on her face.

Overheard by Jemima, The Buttery, Trinity

Posted on Wednesday, 13 April 2005

# Our Lady of Fatima Mansions

Religion teacher: 'Anyone ever hear about the story of an apparition of the Virgin Mary at Fatima?'

Girl: 'Fatima? Wha, ya mean Fatima where the Luas stops?' (referring to the Luas stop at Fatima Mansions)

Overheard by Stephen, Religion class in Dublin school (5th year class)

Posted on Wednesday, 13 April 2005

# Bisexual patients

While visiting the Mater Hospital, hearing an old man complaining about the current conditions in hospital and being kept in a unisex environment:

Old Man (to his daughter): 'I'm 92 years old and here I am being left on a bed in a corridor with all these other patients, and to make it worst it's bisexual!'

Overheard by Bill, Mater Hospital
Posted on Wednesday, 13 April 2005

## Blind ignorance

At the cinema waiting for a friend I began listening to these two lads having a chat about what films they wanted to see.

Lad 1: 'I'd like to see this Ray movie everyone iz on about.'

Lad 2: 'Heard abou that. What's that abou?'

Lad 1: 'Dunno man, think it's about Stevie Wonder or somethin!'

Overheard by nuno, UCI Cinema, Tallaght
Posted on Wednesday, 13 April 2005

# Isaac's index of Irish shares

Heard on the no. 46A into Dublin. Two D4 type girls sitting in front of me.

Girl #1: 'If I wanted to learn about shares, loike, what should I do?'

Girl #2: 'Dunno, maybe find that Isaac guy, my dad is always talking about him and his index of Irish shares.'

Overheard by Pamela, no. 46A bus
Posted on Wednesday, 13 April 2005

# Brother or sister?

I was on the no. 33 bus when I overheard a mother and her son talking about how she was pregnant. The mother turns to her son who was about four and says, 'So, what would you prefer, a sister or a brother?'

And the son replies, 'No, I want a hedgehog.'

Overheard by Lisa, no. 33 bus
Posted on Wednesday, 13 April 2005

# Real rugger bugger

There would often be a question as to whether Leinster rugby fans are REAL rugby supporters. This question was answered at a Leinster home match in Donnybrook when a D4 type standing behind us shouted, 'Come on Orland!'

'Nuff said!

Overheard by partygirl, Donnybrook
Posted on Wednesday, 13 April 2005

# A shed full o' laughs

I was catching an early flight from Dublin Airport and parked in the long term car park. The Aer Rianta bus driver warned us to remove all our personal items. We all listened intently. He finished by saying,

'I'm only tellin' ya dis because I can't fit an'tin more into my shed at home.'

Oh how we laughed!

Overheard by Ronan, Dublin Airport
Posted on Wednesday, 13 April 2005

# Theoretical universe of love

In work a few months back, two lads started talking about the world-famous, wheelchair-bound physicist Stephen Hawkins.

Dude 1: 'Yeah, he's a genius alright and he's really rich, but I read in the paper that his wife beats him stiff.'

Dude 2: 'No way, that's disgraceful!'

Dude 1: 'Yeah, she's really mean to him. I mean why would you want to marry someone just to be horrible to them?'

Dude 2: 'Well if some super-rich dude in a wheelchair wanted to marry me, I'd totally do it! Just call me Mrs Wheelchair.'

Silence ...

Overheard by Jim, in work
Posted on Wednesday, 13 April 2005

# Dublin bus drivers are legends

Some heavy rain during the winter caused floods on roads north out of Dublin. At evening rush hour it took almost three hours to get from the city centre to Santry. The driver of the no. 33 bus kept everybody in good humour by singing songs and cracking jokes. But an impatient Russian builder (obviously not familiar with joviality!) proceeded to give the driver a tongue lashing as he was getting off the bus for causing him to be very late for work (seemingly Dublin Bus controls the weather, which is handy if you don't want to start your route till you've had another cuppa).

The bus driver responds, 'Sure why didn't ye say anything before, if I had a known I would a let ye out to swim.'

Overheard by Anonymous, no. 33 bus
Posted on Tuesday, 12 April 2005

# Flight stimulator

Was watching RTE news at six today. The presenter was talking about the security scare at Dublin Airport. He then turned to this young one 'security expert' in the studio. She explained that some knives and a fake bomb were smuggled through security, before reassuring viewers that it was just a 'stimulated exercise'.

Overheard by Jack, on RTE
Posted on Tuesday, 12 April 2005

# Great mind never bores

At a rather prestigious award ceremony at UCD they had an old alumnus come to talk to a fairly well-to-do audience of Ireland's foremost academic minds. The former student was getting on a bit and despite his respect as a great mind in his field, he was Dublin through and through. As a host for the event I was to walk him on and off stage.

As he was introduced to rapturous applause he turned to me and said in a thick Dublin accent,

'Jaysis, they spent six years trying to kick me out for drinking, fornicating and drinking more and they invite me back 50 years later to say thanks! ... Gobshites the lot of them.'

Not sure what he talked about after that but needless to say he stole the show for me with that line.

Overheard by Sarah, UCD presentation
Posted on Tuesday, 12 April 2005

# Tres witty

I work for a funeral directors firm in Dublin. We assisted an archaeology team at an old inner city church which was clearing the contents of several medieval crypts. The material found was examined and then taken to Glasnevin for cremation. The church is beside Wolfe Tone Park, a well known spot for winos and longterm homeless to spend the day.

As I was carrying one of the containers to our ambulance, one of the drunk lads shouts out,

'Oy, comeer mister, I've a bleedin' bone to pick with you!'

Overheard by Michael, Wolfe Tone Park
Posted on Tuesday, 12 April 2005

# Loose grasp of Geography

In a taxi on the way to the airport, the honest-to-goodness Dublin cabbie engages me in conversation:

Cabbie: 'So off on yer holiers?'

Me: 'Going to a wedding.'

Cabbie: 'Oh yeah? Whereabouts?'

Me: 'Prague.'

Cabbie: 'Prague? Dat's eh ... Budapest, innit?'

Conversation became stilted thereafter ...

Overheard by The Owl, taxi to the Airport
Posted on Tuesday, 12 April 2005

# Give that man a job

Interviewing a few lads for floor staff in wholesalers:

Me: 'What are your main strengths?'

Man: 'I'm very hardworking, brave and above all modest' (I think he meant honest).

Me: 'OK, what are your main weaknesses?'

Man: 'Cryptonite.'

Had to give him the job after that!

Overheard by Batistuta, wholesaler in Fairview
Posted on Tuesday, 12 April 2005

## Young Logic

My 5-year-old sister comes out of Christmas mass
and says to my mam, 'How can he be born at
Christmas if they hanged him at Easter?'

Overheard by Gerry, Clougherhead chapel
Posted on Monday, 11 April 2005

## Weight Watchers

Woman in chipper says to person taking orders,
'Hav ya anythin Low Fat? I'm on a diet.'

Overheard by Shel, Macari's chipper, Dublin
Posted on Monday, 11 April 2005

## People that never died before ...

Two women were talking the other day about a
well-known local who had just died. Visibly
moved and taken aback by the event, the first
woman says, 'Jaysus, it's shocking, the amount
of people dead in the last while.'

And the second says, 'Shocking alright, there's
an awful amount of people dying nowadays that
never died before.'

Overheard by Gaby, Pearse Street
Posted on Monday, 11 April 2005

## Eurovision

I was in the shopping centre the following
morning after the Eurovision, exchanging the
usual banalities with customers, when someone

asks if we saw the Eurovision last night, to which the auld fool says,

'Yeah, same old story, them Latin American countries voting for each other!'

Overheard by Anonymous, Donaghmede Shopping Centre
Posted on Monday, 11 April 2005

## More taxi driver wisdom

I am having a bizarre meandering conversation with your usual header of a taxi driver when he asks me what I study. I tell him Arts in UCD to which he replies, 'Jaysus, sure you artists only earn money after you die!'

Overheard by Mark, Dublin taxi
Posted on Monday, 11 April 2005

## Velcroman

On our way to a Shels match myself and my mates were running for a DART but just missed it (in the typical painful way — doors close just before we got down to the platform). One of my mates (let's call him Velcroman for legal reasons) said:

'Wouldn't it be great if the DART was covered in velcro so when it's pulling out of the station you could jump on and attach yourself' (assuming everyone wears some kind of velcro suit!).

We just couldn't stop taking the mick and then he dug himself even deeper when another of my mates asked how you'd get off. Velcroman's reply was,

'They could employ some guys to stand at each station with big sticks to pry people off.' We couldn't believe it, he was actually serious!

Later, after the match, we again just missed a DART. Velcroman comes up with another ingenious plan:

'OK if you don't like my velcro idea how about one big long DART stretching from Howth to Greystones so you'd never miss one!'

Priceless conversation!

Overheard by Not tonight son, on the way to and from a Shels match
Posted on Monday, 11 April 2005

## Weeta-thicks!

One morning I was after staying in a hotel and I was eating my breakfast and I see an American couple eating weetabix with marmalade on it. Then I hear the couple say to a waitress,

'Your brown bread is very dry. I've heard a lot about your brown bread in America.'

Overheard by anon, a hotel in Dublin
Posted on Monday, 11 April 2005

## Questioning one's omelette management abilities

In Argos one day I overheard a man shouting at the girl behind the counter, saying that he wants a refund. The girl tells him that the manager has already told him that he's not getting his money back. The man replies,

'Your manager? She couldn't manage a f\*\*kin omelette!'

Overheard by Kate, Argos
Posted on Monday, 11 April 2005

## More snob 'location confusion'

One day I was in the dressing rooms in Penneys. I heard someone's phone ringing. A woman with a posh accent answers and starts yappin away! The person on the phone must have asked her where she was:

'Oh, I'm in Atmosphere! It's a store near Debenhams and Morks!'

Overheard by anon, Penneys, Mary Street
Posted on Monday, 11 April 2005

## You've gotta make sure

Was working in a music store and an old enough woman came in and asked, 'Do you sell CDs?'

I pointed her in the direction of ... well ... the whole shop.

Overheard by Edwina, music store
Posted on Monday, 11 April 2005

## Pronunciation is key

Having a pint one Sunday evening, and the conversation at the table next to us gets round to holidays and who's going where. One of the men at the table turns and says,

'I'm going to Majorca (pronouncing it with a J instead of a Y).'

He is immediately corrected by a 'well educated' female friend who is delighted to inform him that it's not madge-orka, but may-orka.

She continues, 'Anyways when are you going?'

To which the guy replies, 'Last week in Yune, first week of Yuly!'

Overheard by Bomber, Kielys, Donnybrook
Posted on Monday, 11 April 2005

## I want a munchkin now, Daddy!

Two girls sitting behind me on the no. 48A bus were reminiscing about the old Willy Wonka film and one of them says,

'What was the name of de little fellas again? Yeh know, de ones dat went Oompa Loompa?'

'Munchkins ya tick!' replied the smart one ...

Overheard by Batterburger, no. 48A bus
Posted on Monday, 11 April 2005